# MAMMA IN HER VILLAGE

Maristella de Panizza Lorch

TBR Books
New York

Copyright © 2020 by Maristella de Panizza Lorch

All rights reserved. No part of this publication may be reproduced, distributed, or transmitted in any form or by any means, without prior written permission.

TBR Books is a program of the Center for the Advancement of Languages, Education, and Communities. We publish researchers and practitioners who seek to engage diverse communities on topics related to education, languages, cultural history, and social initiatives.

>CALEC - TBR Books
>750 Lexington Avenue, 9th floor
>New York, NY 10022
>www.calec.org | contact@calec.org
>www.tbr-books.org | contact@tbr-books.org

Cover Design: Eunjoo Feaster

Front Cover Illustration © Walter Sturn

First published in 2005 by Ruder Finn Press

ISBN 978-1-947626-27-0 (paperback)
ISBN 978-1-636070-27-8 (hardcover)
ISBN 978-1-636070-30-8 (eBook)

Library of Congress Control Number: 2021931519

"The rhythm of *Mamma in her Village* is rapid and sustained. There is no unnecessary word, adjective, or sentence. In fact, there are some pages in which the rhythm becomes tight, marked by short sentences, similes and comparisons that lend tone, until, having reached its climax, the tension relaxes and one feels the urge to reread those pages calmly.

The story is constructed around the theme of the relation between roots, history that changes, and freedom of personal choice. It is in fact the story of free choices grafted on habits rooted in the depth of one's soul.

The entire tale is anchored to the context of one valley in its historical and folkloristic development. I recall my own grandparents' tales [of the Trentino valleys] and I felt as though I were touching, hearing, smelling, as though I were *seeing* it all again (both with my eyes and my imagination). To cover history through concrete people is both interesting and pleasant, but this story also helps elucidate one's own life choices. I devoured the book in two sittings."

Daniela Parisi, Professor of History and Economic Thought, Catholic University of Milan


"Maristella de Panizza Lorch's fictionalized account of her mother's struggles, realizations, learning, and deep loves as a child and young adult growing up in an alpine valley of what is now northern Italy, is captivatingly written. A personal story of extraordinary charm, it is also an account of trial and courage that can inspire and evoke the imagination of any reader in any era. Each character in this book has it unusual strength, each character carries life bravely and with humor. In addition, the book tells the fascinating story of a village trapped by the territorial ambitions of national powers vying for control of Europe before and during World War I. This book is a must read, both because it will touch your heart and because it will feed your hunger for cultural understanding."

Ingrid Bacci, author, *The Art of Effortless Living*

"Maristella de Panizza Lorch's *Mamma in her Village* is a deceptively simple novel. This account of the young adulthood of the author's mother offers a meditation on the bonds of family and the villages we inhabit – physical, temporal, familial – the villages of our own quotidian habits and knowledge, the forms and structures and traditions that define a life. In this idyll, however, Lorch presents the forces of change wrought by history, war, and the passage of time. This tension, as experienced through the eyes of a strong and intelligent woman, lies at the heart of this story. Through spare, economic prose, the author transports the reader to a prewar Europe usually obscured by romance and myth. Maristella Lorch's masterful novel is a clear-eyed look at history, love, and the strength of one woman in the midst of a turbulent era."

    Michael K Dunn, JD, Assistant Vice President of Equity and Inclusion, St. Mary's College of Maryland

"Pina, the protagonist of this engrossing memoir, is an extraordinary woman of fortitude and foresight as is her daughter, Maristella de Panizza Lorch. Luckily for us, Maristella Lorch has chosen to chronicle the history of her mother and her family, a story that sheds light on some of the events in Europe in the run-up to World War I that shaped the everyday lives of those who lived through those times. *Mamma in her Village* tells the story of Pina as a child and young woman in her alpine – now northern Italian – village in the years preceding and during World War I. Lorch not only has a clear understanding of the greater sweep of history but also of its minutiae that lead to personal hardship, heartbreak, and happiness. She has the storyteller's knack for bringing characters to life and pacing the plot so that the reader never loses interest. I did something I haven't done in a long time. I read the book from cover to cover without pause. It was wonderful!"

    Mary Anne Fitzgerald, Journalist, Author, *Nomad: journeys from Samburu*

*To*
*Lavinia*

I dedicate *Mamma in her Village* to my daughter Lavinia. While my mother offered the raw material for the novel, it was Lavinia who justified my writing it with her uninterrupted faith and support. She read and reread all of its various versions offering intelligent advice, and edited its final version.

A Euro-American by education and at heart, Lavinia was inspired since childhood by Laura Ingalls Wilder's very human retelling of a child's personal discovery of the West. When, while rereading as an adult the Little House series to her children, she discovered Mamma's Village in the Alps, Lavinia approached it with the same sense of adventure and discovery with which she had followed the covered wagon across the prairie—a peep hole into a world removed in time and space and yet still within her reach. Her enthusiasm served not only as an inspiration for me; it provided me with the necessary courage to present Mamma's European story to an American public.

New York, January 15, 2004

# Also by Maristella de Panizza Lorch

### OTHER VOLUMES OF THE TRILOGY

*Beyond Gibraltar* (2020);
*The Other Shore* (2019).

### OTHER PUBLICATIONS

Critical edition of Lorenzo Valla's *De Voluptate* (1431-44);
*On Pleasure* (translation of Lorenzo Valla's *De Voluptate*);
*A Defense of Life: Lorenzo Valla's Theory of Pleasure;*
*Folly and Insanity in Renaissance Literature (*with Ernesto Grassi);
Ziliolo's *Michaelida* (1431), editor.

# Geography and History of the Südtirol

Tajo, Mamma's village, lies in the lower Valle di Non or Anaunia, one of the innumerable valleys that crisscross the Central Alps.

Since the end of World War I, the Valle di Non belongs to the most Northern region of the Republic of Italy, the *Trentino/Alto Adige*. When Mamma lived there (1886-1919), that is at the time of our story, the region was part of the Habsburg Empire. By calling it *Südtirol* since the very moment of its official acquisition in 1816, that is by connecting it with the old Austrian territory of the Northern and Eastern Tirol, the Habsburg declared the whole region "Austria," oblivious of the geographical fact that the region lies South of the Alpine watershed.

Today, within an Italy open to the markets of Europe, the Valle di Non, one of the richest of the Alpine valleys, stretches, among high mountains, along the river Noce, like an earthly paradise of pear and apple-orchards laden with fruit. In Mamma's times, as part of the Habsburgic Südtirol, Tajo was poor like the rest of the valley. It did not, however, provide the mines of Pennsylvania or Wyoming with a constant flow of hard-working emigrants, as Cloz or Fruz or Flavon, villages of the Upper Valley, did. Tajo endured its poverty with dignity, perhaps aware, one may be tempted to argue, that sooner or later it would get its chance of revival. It did indeed revive when, by force of World War I, it reacquired its natural connection with the Mediterranean, and mostly since, due to World War II and the end of the Cold War, it acquired a market for its fruit both in the North as well as the South.

§ § §

Geography conditions history. From the night of times, the Central Alps, a section of the chain of the Alps that mark the Northern border of Italy, stood like a sturdy wall protecting Italy from Northern winds and invasions. Climactically, the Südtirol reaps the benefits of its situation simply by being South of the Alpine watershed. Rivers carve out valleys from inside the high mountains, flowing into the

Mediterranean Sea. The wider and hence sunnier the valley is, the warmer the climate. Some Alpine valleys, dells and hollows, if properly irrigated, produce a luxuriant vegetation. That is what happened in recent times with the Valle di Non.

Historically, the region is marked by its geographical situation, a zone of demarcation between the North and the Mediterranean. Rivers and hence valleys are the natural path for penetrating the region. Protected by their natural fortresses, the original population, the Retii, gave the Romans a hard time, until General Drusus in the 1st century A.D. conquered the region by moving up along the river Adige that runs through it. The Valle di Non, in Latin *Anaunia*, was the first section of the area to obtain Roman citizenship in 46 A.D.

From the arrival of the Romans on, the Adige river—*Etch* in German—strongly contributed to the creation of the unique identity of this corner of the Alps, and hence to its history. By crossing the mountainous region from North to South, the Adige, after the second bend rich in slow-moving waters, encouraged the penetration of advanced Mediterranean civilizations. The camps or *oppida* established by the Roman army at the main bends of the Adige easily developed into the region's major cities. From the Upper Adige down, Merano/Meran, Bolzano/Bozen, Trento/Trent witness by their very names their Roman origin as well as a constant German presence.

The Adige seems to have influenced history directly also by force of one its two 'narrows.' The Narrows of Salorno, between Bolzano/Bozen and Trento, favored, in the 9th century A.D. the defeat of the Baiuvari by the Longobards, a fact that cut the Upper Adige region between Bozen and Trento into two linguistically and culturally different zones. The Baiuvari, who descended from Bavaria, like many "barbarians" before them, attracted by the climate and the standard of living of the South, spoke a German dialect. The Longobards who held them back behind the Narrows of Salorno were former "barbarians" who, after a stay in Northern Italy in what is now Lombardy, had adopted Latin as a language and Roman law and culture enriched by Christianity.

The defeat of the Baiuvari by the Longobards at the Narrows of Salorno cut the region of the High Adige in two, like twins joined at the head, held together by the land and river they shared. North of the Narrows of Salorno the Upper Adige or *Alto Adige* spoke a German dialect and gravitated North towards Bolzano/Bozen. The region south of the Narrows that gravitated towards Trento spoke a Latin dialect like the Longobards. The river Noce that carved out the Valle di Non by flowing into the Adige South of Salorno, decided the fate of its inhabitants who fell in the Latin area of Trento.

Besides the Adige, the nature of the mountains and the presence or absence of passes influences the history of the region and privileges communication between certain valleys while isolating others. The main pass, the Brenner Pass, offers the easiest communication between North and South. While the Lower Valle di Non, which includes Tajo, gravitates towards Trento because of the river Noce, the existence of two passes (the Pass of Mendola and the Pass of Le Palade) allowed linguistic and cultural ties to develop between the Upper Valle di Non and the 'German' Bozen.

§   §   §

The current political and economic situation is in part explainable by a millennium of history. During the Middle Ages, the history of the whole Adige area both North and South of the Narrows is characterized by the powerful presence of the Archbishop of Trento who becomes, shortly after the Carolingian period, a *de facto* representative of the German Roman Emperor in the whole region. As a Prince in charge of the whole area South of the watershed, he establishes the Emperor's authority over the feudal lords, first the Counts of Appiano who occupy the fertile zone of the Adige between Trento and Bozen, then, with much more difficulty, over the most powerful Counts of Tirol who dominate the Adige River from their castle over Merano. Language does not play much of a role in those fights. The Duchy of Trento extends at times up to Merano. At times, however, the Counts of Tirol occupy valleys close to Trento, like the Valle di Non. Both the Bishop and the Count vie at this point for the investiture of the German Roman Emperor. The Pope is present only as a guarantee of the ecclesiastical importance of the Bishop whose title of "Prince" derives directly from the Emperor. The Bishop of Trento is like the rest of the nobility of the area, a Ghibelline Prince.

The year 952 is generally considered as the date of the transferal of Trento under Imperial influence. From that moment on and from the following three centuries, Trento becomes "the Emperor's gate to Italy."

In 1363, the last Countess of Tirol, Marguerite Maultasch, who then dominated the region, upon her death leaves the whole area, including Trento, to Rudolph IV of Habsburg. From 1363 on, the Principality of Trento which was secularized, holding at least in appearance, that is, its own authority, becomes the gate to the Habsburg Empire, with only brief intervals during the Napoleonic era. (In 1806, Austria ceded the principality briefly to Bavaria. In 1810 it was for a brief period part of the short-lived Napoleonic Kingdom of Italy. In 1816, the Habsburg made it part of the whole Upper Adige region, which they called the Südtirol.)

During the 19th century, from 1848 on, the Tridentine liberal intelligentsia and Trento's liberal upper classes joined their counterparts on the Italian side of the border in insurrections against the Austrian 'tyrant.' They were severely punished by the Austrian police.

Italy decided to wage war against Austria in part at least because of the failure in the early months of 1915 to reach a diplomatic agreement with Austria concerning its natural geographic borders—the Alpine watershed. In the early months of 1915, Austria was willing to cede only the Italian-speaking territory of the Südtirol, with the exclusion of the Valleys of the Avisio and the Noce. And Austria was unwilling to give up the German-speaking Tirol.

§   §   §

By finally obtaining, at the end of World War I, the whole of the Südtirol — the German as well as the Italian speaking areas above and below the Adige Narrows of Salorno —, Italy inherited the problem of dealing with the interests of two different linguistic areas, a problem with which the Habsburgs had dealt with relative success since 1363. After Mussolini's total failure, at the end of the second World War, the new democratic Republic of Italy reached a possible solution to the problem with the de Gasperi-Grube agreement of

1946. It took the 'Tirolians' over thirty years to have that agreement finally implemented by the United Nations in 1969 as "*il Pacchetto*" ("the Little Package"). Some most valuable efforts on the part, among others, of an Italian Ambassador to Vienna, Angelino Corrias, were made vain by Italian internal politics. The 'Tirolians' themselves, unfortunately, actively contributed to their cause with terroristic acts in addition to all legal means available.

§ § §

Now the area of Bozen, North of the Salorno Narrows, enjoys a form of autonomy that fully preserves its language and culture, while politically it remains part of Italy. The two areas of the old Südtirol, the German speaking "Alto Adige" and the Italian speaking "Trentino," currently enjoy a close cooperation at all levels, the best possible guarantee of their most successful economic development.

A few of the Bishop/Princes of Trento played an important role in Medieval and Renaissance history. Outstanding among them is the Cardinal Bernardus Clesius, Bernard of Cles, the main town of the Valle di Non. A powerful leader as well as an outstanding humanist, a diplomat and personal adviser to the German Emperor, known for his humanistic and legal studies as well as for his love for art and architecture, Bernard of Cles completely changed Trento's architecture and way of life. He subdued a revolution led by his own people of the Valle di Non against the abuses of power of the noblemen and the clergy. In the history of the Church he is well known as one of the organizers of the Council of Trent which met in three intervals between 1545 and 1563 to establish the dogmas of the Catholic Church against the threats of Lutheranism. It seems that, among the 16th century rebels of the Valle di Non, there were a number of Luther sympathizers.

# Contents

Prologue _____ 1
My Village _____ 5
Trento's Cathedral and Its People _____ 21
The Devil _____ 43
At Home in Tajo and Cincinnati _____ 51
A White Rose _____ 75
Sarajevo _____ 89
The War Kills My Village _____ 111
Epilogue _____ 143
About the Author _____ 147
About TBR Books _____ 149
About CALEC _____ 151

# Prologue

Mamma in her Village came to life as a novel thirty years after my then eighty-year-old mother recounted to me her stories on her last visit to us from Rome, in July 1969. Cut off in time and space from the raw "material" of her stories, she freely evoked in her imagination and in her memory, places and characters within the village which she thought would be her home forever…. That is, before a meeting with my future father had projected her into a new world.

As she gradually placed herself on the stage of a world that she had inhabited without him while unconsciously dreaming of 'him,' alongside people and places some of whom I had known from my childhood perspective, I grasped with emotion and awe the miraculous, almost imperceptible moment when the story of an individual, no matter how unimportant in the grand scheme of things, stands poised to flow into the wide, anonymous river of History. *Mamma in her Village* is an attempt to give permanence to that fleeting, yet very real moment, by re-living those stories. Within the "story" of *Mamma in Her Village* a liberated "Mamma" acts and speaks as a child and a young woman, within the freedom the novel allows her.

Mamma was not a storyteller by vocation. For Papa inventing stories was as natural as breathing. He could not live without it. And it is as a storyteller that he survives in my memory; a storyteller who was constantly capable of transforming reality into magic. During the five years we lived together he could solve all my problems with his stories. After Papa's death, Mamma, when pressed, did not dislike telling us children what she called *real* stories: episodes of life in her village, of the war, of her family, of her school, of the noble family that throughout her youth dominated the village and then became her own, of people and places around her. Most of her stories were meant as a homage to her beloved husband. The stories we loved most were those about her village during the first World War. They were scattered, self-enclosed episodes that led nowhere.

When, as a married woman living in America, more precisely in New York's inner City of Columbia University, I asked her one day, during one of her visits from Rome, to tell me freely but chronologically what she remembered about life in her village before my birth, she looked at me embarrassed and amazed. In what way could her own views on life in her village matter to anybody, least of all to me in this moment of my life, when, according to her, I had reached success on all fronts. Life here on this shore of the Atlantic, with a whole continent open to me, was perfect. For her, America personified that 'freedom' she had longed for most of the time unconsciously as she spent the first thirty years of her life in her "Village," that is before she married my father. By this she meant that she was well aware that at the onset of the century life in Tajo, her native village buried in a corner of the impervious Central Alps, was anything but perfect. The house-stewardess of Monsignor Bertolini, Dean of the Cathedral of Trento, defined it 'uncivilized.' Trento, on the contrary, the city where Mamma studied to become a teacher, was the capital of the region called "Südtirol," before 1918 part of the Austro-Hungarian Empire.

§ § §

It took me a long time and some subtle arguments to dismantle her resistance to consider her own stories worthy of being told. Finally, in July 1969, while we were both sitting on a log in our forest in the Catskills, she suddenly asked me if I was still interested in her village. I was delighted, of course. From that moment on, day after day, her stories poured out of her soul, one after the other, wave after wave. I couldn't stop her. As I listened, sitting near her in a secluded corner of a world so unimaginably different from her mountains and her village, yet such as to evoke them in her imagination, I felt as if I witnessed the flowing of a spring into a brook which became a torrent and finally a river. It was a river that slowly and majestically flowed into the ocean of my own life.

Mamma's vision of her village in the heart of the Central Alps was due to the strange, miraculous — for me — interweaving of two contrasting factors: her obsession with 'truth' — as she called factual reality — and her overflowing poetic imagination. Only in the sunset of her life, when illness had eaten away much of her flesh and bones and deprived her of her physical strength, did her poetic imagination, very much alive in her childhood but kept at bay in the most active years of her adult life, find a free outlet. Away from "home," it could finally triumph over that obsessive devotion to 'truth' imposed on her by life in her family and by her profession of school teacher, product of the old-fashioned Austrian educational system.

In July 1969, inspired by the neutral wilderness of our modest old Catskills, as she gradually and imperceptibly entered the enchanted world of her childhood and adolescence, Mamma relived like a child her relationship with her mother and father, with her goats and the villagers. With the peevish curiosity of a bright young girl she revisited the role played in the village and in the valley by my father's family of which she was destined to become a part. A new kind of truth surfaced then from her stories, a truth of which she had been unaware throughout her life.

"What is 'truth,' mamma, anyway?" I asked her one day, before she finally decided to open the 'story book' she had kept hidden from me all of her life.

"Truth are facts as they really happened. Truth is history," she replied.

"What you are telling me, mamma, is far better than what you call 'history.' It is life as you lived it. I saw you living part of it, but I missed out on the best, on what came before you gave birth to me." Mamma had been a high-school teacher most of her life, obsessed during my childhood with teaching me 'history' when all I wanted to do was to read novels. History for Mamma was a list of names of 'Great Individuals,' — Alexander the Great, Charlemagne, Napoleon, a few heroes of the war of Italian independence. They were names corresponding to dates, plenty of dates, and to places that were to be identified on the Atlas. The list did not include Mussolini nor King Victor Emanuel III, his 'partner,' as she called him. All names, dates and events were to be learned by heart. She used to get angry at me because I did not distinguish the Assyrians from the Egyptians, Tutankhamun from Assurbanipal. I owed it to her and to my first history teachers if for a long time I hated history books and stubbornly stuck to novels. Homer and Tolstoy helped me to overcome the impasse. What helped her, I suppose, was life itself, as she moved on, after her husband's death, with bankruptcy and four young children to raise, trying boldly to make a place for herself and her children not among 'the Great' but among the people she loved and respected.

In that Catskillian July she smiled at me, as if she remembered the fights we had had on the subject. So I held in my arms her frail, tiny body, destroyed by osteoporosis, and kissed her and begged her not to waste precious time discussing the value of the stories I asked her to tell me.

"What happened to you in your village, what did your village look like when you lived in it, light years away from where we live right now, matters more to me, I said, than what I can read about in all the history books in the world! And there is only one person who can tell me this story. That person is you."

I had known mamma for many years as an astonishingly strong woman, capable of breath-taking decisions, a woman who subjected herself and her children to a spartan discipline and continuously exacted 'sacrifice' (a common word in our family vocabulary) in order to reach certain goals that *she* had set for the family. It was painful for me to see that very same woman now smile at me wistfully like a child and give in to my request without objecting. That childish smile, however, was soon replaced by a gentle expression of dignified consent.

"Some of the stories I am about to tell you will make your children laugh." she said.

It was shortly after that meeting of hearts that Mamma with one leap jumped over the Rubicon.

§    §    §

*I have kept Mamma as the narrator in my own novel which is freely based on the stories she told me.*

# CHAPTER 1

## My Village

In the season when the snow melts and the grass turns green, as the first beams of light brighten the sky, the bells of Saint Mary ring the *Ave Maria*. Then we all know that the guardian of our goats, a thin willowy boy with sleepy eyes, is there in the grassy square waiting to collect our goats for the pastures. The sound of his trumpet followed by his loud voice is heard through the whole village. "Come, friends, bring me your goats. Don't make me wait." The priest at the altar in the very old church of Santa Maria sings in a deep voice the *Ave Maria*.

I know today is my chance to get away from home. I quietly slide out of Mare's huge bed before she and Pare wake up, but she catches me with one of her strong hands. "Where do you think you are going, *puta*? Don't you know today it's your turn to wash the laundry at the Falls?" The Falls, down the steep gorge of the Noce, is where the families in the village take turns washing their laundry once a week. Then she releases the pressure on my arm. I am free to lead our two goats to Saint Mary.

When I get to the little square, there are many farmers under the linden trees and many goats. The farmers deliver their goats to the boy and leave for the fields. When I am lucky, like today, I can wander up to the prairies under the mountains, alone with the goats.

§ § §

My village is made of poor farmers who have very few animals. We raise mostly goats, very few among us have a cow. That's why I love goats.

It wasn't always like that. My mother's family, called Fuganti, had two oxen. They were among the most respected families in the village. Her mother, Margherita Bazzochera, was the village counselor. Nobody bought or sold anything without asking her for advice. Among her children, two sisters, Lucia and Orsola, married two brothers, that is two Fuganti girls married two Cristoforetti boys to enhance the family's property.

Mother Orsola, *Mare* for me, was so tall that we, her children, could have hidden under her skirt. But we didn't because she always smelled of urine. Mostly because we were afraid of her. We always addressed her with 'thou.' Or never addressed her at all. We answered very politely when she addressed us.

Mare had four daughters and two sons. I was the youngest daughter. Virginia, Emma and Maria had long braids, Virginia had blond hair and blue eyes like Mare, Emma pitch black eyes and hair like Pare, Maria and I were in between our two elder sisters, with light brown hair and green eyes. Every morning, Mare would braid our hair so tight it would hurt to turn our neck, and then warn us with a stern voice: "Don't you dare touch your hair. Or else…." The boys, Damiano and Silvio, went to work in the fields and in the whip factory. We saw the boys only at meals. The meals were just one course, at breakfast *mosa*, a thick white cereal, at lunch *polenta*, at dinner more *mosa*. We could have two servings of everything. There was no wheat in our valley. So we made bread with corn and barley. We made coffee with chicory. We had meat when we killed a chicken or a goat, but that was rare. I remember one family in the village had a pig. We had no electricity and no running water in the house. Candles and water were a most precious commodity.

Pare was not tall, had very dark hair, dark eyes, dark skin. Like many farmers in the village, he had spent years as a worker in Africa. That's why they called him Pero Moro, Peter the Moor. He was so handsome that Siora Maria Panizza, when she came to spend the summer in the village from the capital city of Trento, happily walked down from her mansion to the *pont* of our home huddled with the other houses in the village for protection, because Pare sat there praying. Our house, she said, was blessed by the presence of Pare. Siora Maria settled comfortably facing him. She always asked Mare for permission to paint a portrait of her husband.

"Orsola, she said smiling, don't you know you have as a husband the most handsome man in the village? Moreover, they say he is a saint." Mare would bite back harshly: "It may be as you say, Siora. Go ahead and paint, but I sure wish he could be of more help around here. We don't have enough hands to work and we have more than enough mouths to feed...."

Pare kept on praying while Siora Maria painted his portrait for her collection, which none of us saw, and Mare laughed, which happened rarely.

Our day ended after sunset with the darkening of the sky. Goats were already in the stables. By then we had brought in, balancing them with a long *bazilon* on our shoulders, two huge copper basins of water from the village fountains, our water supply for the night. When the church bell rang the *Angelus*, Mare and Pare knelt near the big porcelain stove in the *Stua*, with us all around them, and we sang the *Angelus* and recited the rosary. Then we all went to bed. I, the youngest, would sleep in the *Stua*, in the big bed of dry corn leaves, between Mare and Pare, which was so nice and warm in the winter. At night we did not pee in the out-house but in a chamber pot which we pushed under the bed. It was hard for me to move it when Mare and Pare had used it before me.

§ § §

Life in our village was as peaceful as sleeping in bed with Mare and Pare. Since everybody around us was equally poor, every fight was easily settled. We all contributed, for instance, without squabbling, the food for the goat herder. If someone was in trouble, because of an illness or childbirth or a death or a worm in the vines, we went for help to the parish priest. Pare's family matched the family of Mare in reputation. His brother was a priest. The priest of the village could turn for help to Trento, a city of High Priests governed by the Bishop who was a Prince of the Church.

§ § §

The most immediate support, however, came to our village not from the priest, the Bishop, the Emperor or the Pope, but from Sior Augusto and his family, the de Panizza Inama von Brunnenwald, for us the Siori Panizza.

Sior Augusto, the leader of the family, was the best lawyer in the region of Südtyrol and a representative of our district in Vienna. If we in the Valley had some complaint he was the one who took it to the Emperor.

Yet he did much more than that. He saw to it that Tajo had what it needed to live as he thought it should live as a 'civilized community.' First, for us came the Church. Thus he paid for the painting at the main altar and for the Italian marble of the altar itself. (Although he was not Italian, he personally knew everybody who was anybody in Italy.) Second for us in importance came our dead. Before his time we used to bury them in or around the church. For the official cemetery of Tajo Sior Augusto chose a secluded plot outside the village near a little wood fragrant with the perfume of wild cyclamens. There he put his own dead to rest and we followed his example. He housed a kindergarten in one of his two homes, the huge stone castle-like mansion which overlooked the village surrounded by orchards and vines, embraced by a forest.

§   §   §

The miracle of that forest was a spring. In the thickest and most secluded corner of the forest a few drops of cool water leaped gently out of a thick layer of moss. They peered out of the velvety soft emerald, smiling peevishly as we girls smile, blushing, when we meet boys. Then, a little at a time, a full-fledged spring found its way into the world of the sun and the moon and the stars. A flow of cool water, a real spring, searched for the proper path through which to flow and in so doing expanded into many rivulets that gently gurgled, like little birds in their nest when mother bird feeds them. Finally, the spring courageously moved away from its birthplace, away from the emerald soft moss and the protective shadow of the high trees. I hated to see it go because I knew the brook would flow into a torrent and the torrent into the Noce River, which left our valley forever to flow into a river I had not seen, called Adige, which flowed into the *sea*. The sea is like paradise, a place which you cannot imagine and, therefore, it may not even exist. I hated to see my beloved spring lost in paradise.

One of the miracles of that spring was that the soft velvety moss it wetted with its cool water overflowed in the springtime with wild violets. From its long thin fragile stem each little violet looked around with its clear blue eyes, curious. It seemed to me to know what existed beyond the secluded corner of the world where it was born, in the world of the sun. So, after having sat down near those violets for a long time listening to the song of the water, I picked as many violets as I could. (There were always many more left in place.) Of course, I would have liked to take them home, and put them in a vase in a corner of the house where I could look at them during the day when I was free from chores — which happened rarely. But I brought them instead straight to church, because Mare would say she didn't want stolen flowers in her home and would send me up to the Panizza mansion to return them to the owner. So I placed the violets in church under the protection of the Virgin Mary who seemed to me the best company they could find. The Virgin was born in a far-away place near the sea and she was now in paradise. She could tell my violets plenty of stories about the wide world that stretched beyond the other side of the high mountains that protected us from it like a wall.

§ § §

Everybody in Tajo knew that the Emperor in Vienna gave the Siori Panizza the name 'von Brunnenwald' because they had been very useful and good to him. By calling them "those who came from the forest with the spring," the Emperor pointed to the very first place where the family of the Siori was born. They must have leaped out of the earth one day suddenly, I thought, like that marvelous spring. But that happened a long, long time ago, much before the plague and all the wars our old people could remember. What the Emperor meant by giving the Siori an extra name was that he liked them very much, as much as we liked them. This is what I thought.

§ § §

Sior Augusto was the most important person for us in the village, after the Emperor, of course, and the Pope. But Emperor and Pope lived, like God, in far-away places such as Vienna and Rome that we would certainly never see in our lives, whereas Sior Augusto was with us when we needed him, in Tajo. Sior Augusto was the Inspector who chose the teachers for our School which for him was even more important than the church. He was the Judge who decided on all disputes. He began all his speeches by saying that it was Justice and Law that allowed us to live together without killing one another. I don't know why he said that because we never harmed one another in any way. In sum, he was, like Avvocato Mendini and the parish priest and the pharmacist, but much more than they, the wisest man in the village.

Sior Augusto walked through the bumpy paths of the village like a benevolent king, tall and slim and dressed in black. Limping was very befitting to him because it allowed him to lean like an Emperor on a beautiful stick with a golden pummel. He had a long face, a long white beard and long white hair beautifully mixed in with his flowing white beard. When he gave his speeches on a podium built for special occasions in the main square one thought of God in Heaven because his words flowed from his mouth like honey into the heart of all of us who listened. Like God in Heaven, he never smiled, nor did he play or joke, whereas the pharmacist and the parish priest played *bocce* in the shadow of Santa Maria.

We children stood still when we met Sior Augusto on the streets of Tajo and reverently greeted him in *noneso*: "God save you, Sior Augusto." He answered in Italian with a strong, clear, mellow voice, the voice of the priest when at the end of the Mass says to the audience: *Ite, missa est* ("Go, the Mass has ended"), "God save you, my children!" Like in church with the priest, we didn't dare to budge until he was out of sight.

Siora Maria, his wife, was just the contrary of Sior Augusto. Siora Maria, a tiny lady dressed in colorful silk, pirouetted in her silk shoes on our bumpy roads, balancing her palette and colors on one shoulder and on the other a big bag with all sorts of goodies for us children and the old and the sick of the village. She knew all of us kids by name and invited us to follow her. And when she stopped somewhere to paint we gathered around her and she told us the most beautiful stories about knights and princesses who lived once upon a time hidden in the rocks around the village. It seemed to me then, while listening to her, that once upon a time there were very few normal people like us in Tajo. Most were knights and monsters and princesses, and poor girls like me always stood a chance, like Cinderella, of becoming a princess.

"I hope I got you well scared" she would laugh after she finished a scary story. Then she added: "Do not bother about learning German in school, but for God's sake learn Italian and become civilized." Her two girls, Clodia and Gemma, were not as funny and amusing as their mother. In winter, they accompanied her from house to house like black shadows, each wrapped in a black cloak sprinkled white with snow. Led by their mother they brought soup to the sick or clothing for a new born baby. Every woman in the village laughed with Siora Maria. Her laughter was irresistible.

I don't know why we loved Siora Maria so much. We loved her even if she did not go to church at all except for big occasions. Even if she made fun of the Bishop in Trento and said our parish priest was better than him... Even when she made fun of the Emperor in Vienna and sang a funny song about him while she was working at a painting of our women washing at the fountain. "Come on" she spurred the women on, "sing with me!"

The women blushed and continued washing.

"What's wrong with that Siora?," they would mutter in *noneso* among themselves. "She never takes herself seriously."

§ § §

Nobody, not even the very old, remembered the village without the Siori Panizza. They had been with us forever with their mansions, their gardens, their parties. People said they were *rich*. But I did not understand what that meant and what it had to do with us. People said all the vines in the valley belonged to them, except for those few fields that belonged to us farmers.

Mare told me one day that the Siori Panizza owned most of the land and took money away from us. She was not angry about it. For her it was a fact of life, not an injustice. Do you get angry at the Emperor in Vienna when his officials come to exact the taxes? I was puzzled about it. Why did the Siori Panizza exact money from us if what they did for the village was a gift? Perhaps Mare was wrong, I thought at first. But one day while the goat herd and I were up at the *spiazzoi,* the steppe-like grounds where we pastured our goats, sitting in the cool shadow of the first gawky trees of the wood that separated Tajo from the next village, Coredo, I got proof that Mare was right, as usual. Yes, the Siori Panizza took money from us.

The heavy silence of a hot summer afternoon was suddenly broken by loud laughter. Three young men on horseback crossed like lightning the dusty steppe where our goats pastured. Both the goat herd and I recognized them as the three young Siori Panizza: Tullio the oldest, fat and clumsy, Antonio the portrait of his father, il Sior Augusto, without his noble qualities, and Gino the youngest, for years a well-known playboy in the valley.

We hardly ever saw Tullio and Antonio around the village. Gino, instead, could be seen through the years when he was younger playing with our boys during the long summer evenings in the Church square. Then he used to squat near the girls who quietly knitted, sitting on the doorsteps of the main Church, one near the other like swallows at sunset. He teased the girls, speaking in *noneso* like them, and he made them all blush — all except me.

"You are too fat to please the girls," I said to him one evening. When he motioned to catch me, I ran straight to my favorite tree in the near-by square of Santa Maria, and before he could reach me I had climbed to the top of it. He looked at me up in the tree and broke out in a hearty laughter, the same laughter as Siora Maria: "Don't worry," he said, "I'll get you somehow, some day…."

"How," I retorted, "since you are too fat to climb trees?"

"I'll get you in this church as my wife."

That evening, after prayers, when we all sat quietly on the *pont,* I told Mare about the joke. She frowned and warned me. "Stay away from that boy. He spells trouble."

§   §   §

"Here they go, the three young Siori Panizza," said my friend the goat herd, "to collect the *decima* ("tithe") in Coredo."

"What is the tithe?" I asked.

He looked surprised at my ignorance and explained: "It is the tenth part of what we own." And he added, laughing: "I don't own anything, but your parents own two goats and two small fields. So you pay."

"And if we don't have the money to pay?"

"Then they take away your fields."

"Who are THEY?"

"The Siori Panizza, of course."

The three young men disappeared in the forest without paying any attention to us or to our goats.

§ § §

Even if we had to pay the tithe, it was fun to live in Tajo. In the morning after work, we went to school most of the day for most of the year every day until we were fourteen. Then, during the summer there was theater performed in the main square in front of the church, comedies recited by the pharmacist and the doctor and the people from Trento who came to our village on vacation.

At the time of the elections there were lively meetings to choose our representatives for the parliament in Vienna. We farmers belonged to the clerical party, the party of the Church and the Emperor, Sior Augusto and Siora Maria to the National Party which did not agree with the Church and the Emperor on many issues. This was cause for much debate. The Siori themselves were divided on the subject of the Church, the Pope and the Priests, the Emperor and the King of Italy. Sior Augusto and Siora Maria stood openly for what they called liberal thinking, which meant disregard for the Bishop and the Pope and the Emperor and leaning towards an atheist government like the one of Italy. Sior Augusto's sisters, Siore Erminia and Clementina, whom people said were once nuns in a convent in Austria and were so religious they attended at least one

Mass a day, believed, like us farmers, that we should all live as God-fearing people. And we should be respectful of the Bishop and the Emperor and let the Italians simmer in their broth, poor and disobedient as they were to the law and to God, spending their time singing instead of working.

§ § §

Everybody in the village knew that Siora Erminia and Siora Clementina had hurried to the side of their brother, Sior Augusto, after he had married that Italian Baroness Ciani, that is Siora Maria, who gave him six children one after the other, without having the faintest idea of how to raise them. Siora Maria warmly welcomed her sisters-in-law as part of her household, grateful that they would relieve her of an ungrateful responsibility.

The two pious sisters began by having the children baptized with no resistance whatsoever from Siora Maria. Then, as the children grew up, the pious sisters saw to it that the two girls be sent to an enclosed cloister, a *convento di clausura*. As for the boys, Siora Erminia, a true saint, who, like all saints was in delicate health and therefore had to spend her winters in Rome with the Pope, took Stefano, the sweetest of the brood, with her to Rome. Little Stefano gave all signs of premature sainthood, but, given the bad sanitary conditions of Rome, he caught typhoid fever and died. Sior Augusto decided then he would take care of the other three boys himself. Tullio, Antonio, and Gino made it with some difficulty to finish the local high school. Then they wandered from university to university in Graz, Munich, and Vienna, having an excellent time but with little academic success, until Gino finally succeeded in earning a degree in law from the University of Vienna. Gino then became the pride and joy of his father. He had always been his mother's favorite: the two resembled each other like two drops of water, with one difference: Gino did not paint.

Whatever happened within the residence of the Siori Panizza was common knowledge in the village, at times even before it happened. Not only at the time of elections, but all throughout the year, women at the public fountain entertained themselves by adding more and more details to juicy stories. My brothers told me they heard some at the village pub. Only Mare was adamantine on rejecting all kind of gossip. We had no right — she told us at home — to look into the private business of Siora Maria, not even when it came to sending our representatives to Vienna. Mare disagreed with her about the role of the church and many other things. But this had nothing to do with the way she and her husband raised their children.

It was hard, Mare explained to us sharply, to accept the crazy ideas of Sior Augusto and of his wife in politics. How could she agree on their unconditional love for the Italians — when everybody knew that the Italians suffered from poor education, heavy taxes, bad bureaucracy and a crazy politics against the Pope in favor of the atheists. How could she agree on disobedience to the Emperor in Vienna?

But how could she not be more than grateful to Sior Augusto and his family for the help they gave her and her family in the affairs of everyday life which are the only thing that counted for us poor farmers. When my beautiful sister Virginia, at twenty, in the heart of a cold December, lay in bed so sick with pneumonia she could hardly breathe, who got a doctor for her but Sior Augusto? And it was Siora Erminia who helped Mare to wash and dress Virginia's beautiful body after she died and closed the coffin over her. Mare turned her head away without a tear in her eyes.

§   §   §

After Virginia died, Pare kept on praying as usual, but Mare stopped speaking altogether for a long time. It was Siora Erminia who came down to our house every day until Mare could speak to us again. We didn't understand how she performed the miracle. From that moment on, Siora Erminia was very close to us and Mare trusted her and listened to her advice. And she never mentioned again the politics of her brother Sior Augusto and of her sister-in-law, Siora Maria, for fear of hurting the feelings of Siora Erminia who didn't agree with them either.

My sister Virginia was as beautiful as an angel. Tall and blonde like Mare, and sweet and quiet like Pare. Home was not the same after she died. It was as if the sun had set on our lives. Nobody dared to mention her name any more except in the morning and evening prayers, for fear that Mare would stop talking again. So we turned to Pare for comfort, and he did what he could to help us. He made us pray with him as a way, I guess, to lead us close to Paradise, until he himself silently joined her.

§    §    §

It was a warm evening in October. Pare sat on the *pont*, his hands crossed as usual in prayer. We never disturbed him when he was like that. That evening, Mare decided she needed his help.

"Come on, Pero," she said, "I need your help with the hay."

Pare didn't budge. She came close to him and shook him slightly. He fell to the floor. Mare raised his light body in her strong arms and laid it gently like a child on their bed in the *Stua*. Then she knelt near him without saying a word, and I and the girls with her. She did not cry. She looked into his face for a long time. Then she turned to my eldest sister Emma: "Go," she said, "to the whip factory and call the boys. You, Maria, go to the parish and call the priest...."

She finally looked at me. I had sunk lifeless at the foot of Pare's bed, terrorized that Pare would be taken away from us like Virginia, locked in a coffin. She smiled at me:

"Get up," she told me gently, "and get some water. We'll wash him and prepare him together."

We undressed him before his limbs became stiff and washed him gently like a baby. He had a very delicate, soft, olive-colored skin like Saint Sebastian in church, and his face looked gray like the face of Christ dead, lying in Mary's lap on the big altar.

When Don Beppe, the Parish priest, arrived with our boys from the factory, we all knelt on the rough floor of the *Stua* and recited the prayer for the dying (although Pare had been dead for quite a while), and Don Beppe told us he would be among the first to resurrect in the Valley of Josaphat because he was a Saint. Then Mare went to the cellar to get some wine for the priest and while he was drinking she held on tight to my hand.

She never let go of me from that moment on for many years. She wanted me to help the family in a different way than the others. She also helped me more than the others by singling me out among all her children "to give me an education."

She did not come to that decision all on her own nor did she ask for my consent. When she took it, however, she stuck to it with the same stubborn obstinacy and enterprising spirit with which she had once saved the house from the creditors and had kept all of us children not only alive but well fed and working from the age of six on, when the rest of the village risked starving and many of the village boys spent time in the pub instead of working in the factory or the fields.

Mare's tragic defeat in life, from which she never recovered, was the death of Virginia. Virginia was a Real Saint, I mean a saint that Mare and all of us could understand. Life was never the same for all of us in the family after God took Virginia with Him, that is away from us to whom she belonged. Pare, Mare used to say, belonged in Paradise. He lived down here in temporary exile.

§ § §

With Pare's death, however, we soon discovered the family had the hardest time to survive. The village — Mare remembered having heard it from her Mother, Margherita Bazzochera — had never starved in spite of droughts and floods and plagues. God had saved them from war so far which is, together with the earthquake, the most fearful disaster that could befall man in our valley.... Since the earth was poor and rocky, the people of Tajo again and again had taken up new initiatives to increase the poor income of agriculture. At one point, they had started to raise silkworms, and Mare remembered how her own grandmother and aunts stayed in bed for weeks to help the larvae of the silkworm warm up in order to accelerate the spinning of the cocoons from which silk is made. That initiative lasted until the Italians across the border produced better silk. Then a group of industrious men started a whip factory. Unfortunately, the moment came when stage-coaches were being used only in the side valleys like the Valle di Non. Down where the Noce river flows into the Adige, between Trento and Bolzano, there was now a horseless carriage, a monster called in Italian *treno* for which there was no word in *noneso*. With the appearance of the puffing monster, there was of course less and less demand for whips.

We were then forced to turn back to the earth and try to squeeze from our fields enough staple to survive. Pare, while he was still with us, Mare, Damiano, one year older than me, and Silvio, two years younger, got up at four in the morning during the months of the sun and went to the fields. Since the fields were far from the village, we had to borrow at times a cow or an ox to pull our cart. Emma, who was tall and lanky but not strong, could hardly help them, and Maria, who was short and stout, did so against her will. So I, who never grew tall and strong like the rest of my family but enjoyed working in the fields, accompanied them most of the time. I was excused only when I went to pasture the goats. And, of course, when I went to school.

School was the joy of my life. School and running free with our goats up at the edge of the big forest, lying on the grass and listening to the chirping of the crickets. Yet school was still the best.

In Mare's time, there was a woman paid by the village to teach in her own home whoever could afford to be taught. Mare had been taught by the parish priest and she had personally taught Pare to read and write shortly after they had married.

School was the most important place in the village after the Church, also because Sior Augusto wanted it to be so. It was located in two big rooms in the Town Hall. We all sat on small benches that had been manufactured by the carpenters in the village. There were two teachers, a man for the big boys and a woman for the girls and the small boys. Our teacher had been taught by her older sister who had had three months of schooling in Trento, the capital of the region.

Our teacher was an old woman always dressed in black. Perhaps she was not so old, but to us she looked older than Methuselah. Everything was black about her, especially her humor. She always seemed to be angry, especially if one of us laughed. We could only giggle covering our face with a hand. I loved a boy behind me. His name was Toni, and he knew how to giggle best of all. Teachers, like nuns, never got married.

Our teacher obeyed God and the Emperor. She had promised both we would learn the Gospel, learn to count and perform the four operations, and write in a straight line more than one line at a time. If we didn't obey and learn, the teacher would order us to put our hands out and she would hit them hard with a stick. While she hit us, she looked happy because she knew next time we would learn.

I was the best in everything, the letters and the numbers. Moreover, I could read the map hanging on the wall under the Crucifix behind the teacher's desk. I could easily point to the Noce River, to Trento, to Innsbruck, and to Vienna, I mean all the places that mattered to us. Of course, there was also Rome, where the Pope lived and the North Pole where everybody freezes and a big chunk of land painted mainly in pink which was called Africa where Pare once went to work and came back black like everybody there because of the hot sun. That's why in the village they called Pare *Pero Moro* ("Peter the Moor"). We believed that only the Missionaries who go to Africa to baptize the blacks are allowed by God to remain white like us.

In school, we had to have clean hands, a clean apron, and clean language. That is, the teacher did not speak our language, *noneso*, but a cleaner language — Italian. All the learning of numbers and letters was in Italian. Sometimes the teacher made the effort to teach us in German. But German was so different from everything we said in our lives, that even the teacher did not seem to understand why she had to go through the effort. Only the Emperor spoke German and perhaps the Bishop in Trento and Sior Augusto, but Siora Maria laughed and said we should forget about German, a language of barbarians. At home, we spoke only our own language, *noneso*, but the priest and the mayor spoke like the teacher, in Italian.

§ § §

I liked the school in Tajo and I never dreamt of any other school in any other place in the big world painted in beautiful colors on the map hanging under the Crucifix behind the teacher's desk. I didn't want to ever, ever, leave my school and my village. Yet something happened that forced me to leave.

# CHAPTER 2

## Trento's Cathedral and Its People

"Cornelia, my sister Clementina's daughter is getting married to...", I overheard Siora Erminia whispering to Mare while I was weeding the cabbages in the garden under the *pont*.

During the summer after Pare's death, Siora Erminia came to visit Mare every evening at sunset, that is after Mare came back from the fields, washed up and had dinner with us, before the church bells rang the *Angelus*. They both sat at the place where Pare used to sit, on the *pont* overlooking the steep gorge of the torrent Noce and, on the other side, the castle of the village Nano, within whose broken-down walls fairies meet every fall, as Siora Maria would tell us children. Siora Erminia and Mare however did not pray. They chatted incessantly.

One hot evening in July Siora Erminia was whispering to Mare. Evidently, it was to be a secret between the two she didn't want us to hear.

Siora Erminia and her sister-in-law, Siora Clementina, were as different from each other as night and day. Yet they were both very good to us in different ways and we loved them both. Siora Erminia was tall and thin as a wafer. She walked like the Queen of Heaven, with short delicate steps, hardly touching the ground, her eyes downcast, her lips lightly moving in prayer. She always dressed in black shining silk, a black lace veil over her white hair which she wore tightly pulled into a knot over her small round head. She always kept a black rosary hanging from her thin waist and recited her beads all day long as if she were husking peas, while she moved around the village, incessantly helping people in need. Now she had decided to help Mare in whatever her needs were. Siora Erminia was more a nun than a Siora. At times, I thought she was perhaps a Saint.

From bits and pieces of the conversation between Mare and Siora Erminia that summer evening on the *pont* I gathered that the most incredible things were happening in the household of Sior Augusto. What did we have to do with it, I asked myself, and why was Mare so interested? A bit of an answer came only at the very end.

§ § §

Mare was reminded that Siora Erminia's sister, Siora Clementina, had married years before into a family "higher up" than the Siori Panizza, the Barons Taxis. Siora Clementina was now, I heard it clearly spelled, the Baroness Clementina Taxis. The Taxis were people so important in Vienna they could even dine with the Emperor if they wanted. I could hardly believe that, because for me the Siori Panizza were the highest of all. But it must have been true, if Siora Erminia, who was a member of the family, said so. The Siori Panizza needed money, so Sior Augusto had arranged a marriage between one of his three sons and his own niece Cornelia, the daughter of Baroness Clementina, who, besides being his sister was also a Baroness which meant she had money. His first choice was the most handsome and charming of his sons, the youngest, Gino, who had recently succeeded in getting his law degree and was destined to work in his father's law firm.

At this point, Siora Erminia lowered her voice to the point that what reached me in the cabbage patch was just a whisper, with Mare sighing so loudly I thought she was sobbing. I then tiptoed cautiously from the cabbage patch to the corn and finally I managed to hide among the tall sunflowers which were almost under the *pont*. Now I could hear everything Siora Erminia said. And was amazed at what I heard. Sior Gino had not only refused to marry his cousin, the Baroness, but had subsequently been banished from the family. I wished I could have seen Siora Erminia's face because her voice was at this point like the moaning of a wounded bird. She loved her Gino dearly, after Stefano of course, who had died in her arms in Rome. And in the twilight, I could see that Mare was holding her hand.

Suddenly, the Church bell began ringing the *Angelus* and the two ladies knelt in prayer. In order for me to kneel I had to leap away from the sunflowers and the corn. But, alas, from that spot I could hear only half of what they said after they stopped praying. What I made out was that Sior Augusto had decided his eldest son Tullio, the plump one, would marry the Baroness.

There was a pause. Then Siora Erminia announced with a normal voice that the marriage would take place soon in Trento and people from all over, that is from Trento and elsewhere, would attend, and the Bishop would officiate.... A great ceremony, a great crowd.... This would be the much-waited-for occasion to approach Monsignor Bertolini, a saintly man, first aid to the Bishop, unfortunately old and sick. Emma... I couldn't make up the rest. Yet, the name of Emma was pronounced clearly more than once in the rest of the conversation.

Hearing the name of my eldest sister, my heart started beating so violently I had to hold it with both my hands on my breast.

I thought at first Emma, like Cinderella, would marry a prince. But how could that be? Emma was a very good girl, but not graceful at all, and certainly not the type to go to a ball even if her fairy godmother had brought her a stunning dress of velvet and lace. Besides, Emma had enormous feet....

That night, having fallen asleep with great difficulty, I dreamt of Emma dancing with Sior Gino under the linden tree in the square of the old church of Santa Maria, while the Bishop looked on, holding the thin white hand of Siora Erminia. My first thought as I woke up was: why was Sior Gino banished from the family? What did he do to deserve such a punishment? Did he simply refuse to marry the baroness?

§ § §

The truth about Emma's role in Siora Erminia's plan surfaced the next day, which was Sunday, clean and neat, like the water of the spring in the forest.

In the early afternoon of that hot Sunday in July, when the crickets chirp wildly and the farmers loaf on their *ponts*, Siora Erminia and Siora Clementina paid us an official visit. Mare had organized everything ahead of time. We received them in 'the room in the middle,' the living room of sorts which was opened only for baptisms and marriages when they did not take place in bad financial times.

The room, whose window opened on a meadow with fruit-trees we called *cesura*, was furnished with a blue velvet sofa, two armchairs and four chairs. A handmade rug covered part of the rough wooden floor, a big mirror hung behind the sofa flanked by a picture of Mare and Pare at their marriage, Mare sitting on a low chair to allow Pare to seem taller than her. In a corner, there was a huge green porcelain stove.

As we entered, a whiff of mold overwhelmed me, like when Mare took me to the cellar. But the window was open and a light breeze caressed the white lace curtain. I had the feeling that a show was about to take place in front of my eyes like magic. I was spell bound.

Siora Erminia was asked by Mare to sit on the sofa with Baroness Clementina on her right. They were both dressed like twins in shining black silk, but the Baroness looked less a Queen than Siora Erminia, although she had pearls and earrings and rings with diamonds. She was younger than her sister. One could guess immediately she had a very minor role to play. She was there only to support Siora Erminia.

Mare sat in one armchair and Emma in the other. They both wore their black dress of coarse hand-woven wool. Maria and I, both dressed like Emma, sat on two chairs that Mare had placed side by side at a distance from Emma's. The two boys, Damiano who was fifteen and Silvio thirteen, were locked in the kitchen and told by Mare to keep perfectly quiet.

I had never seen anything like that before in my own home. It was like a scene for the summer theater put up by the pharmacist in the church square, except now we were the actors in the play. I was lost in contemplation of the mirror — I had never seen one so big before — which reflected all that black on blue, when Siora Erminia broke the silence. I think everybody had been silently praying except for me and Maria who were anxiously waiting for the curtain to rise and the show to start. Maria was a mischievous, down-to-earth girl who was always looking for ways to escape from work.

While she spoke, Siora Erminia held her black rosary in her lap with hands that were as white as snow, as was her face and her hair under the black silk hat.

"Pare, God rest his soul, is now with your saintly sister Virginia among the angels and the archangels where he belongs, and we are left here alone to fare with their help but, to the best of our strength, in this valley of tears...."

She raised her eyes to the beautiful chandelier hanging from the ceiling which I noticed only at that moment.

Having started almost hesitantly, the Siora ran through the rest of the speech as we do in school when the teacher makes us memorize a piece.

"The whip factory is about to close, because horse driven carriages are getting rare. Soon the two boys in the family, Damiano and Silvio, will be laid off and will have hardly enough work for themselves taking care of your three fields.... We have all been cursed, as you know, with the phylloxera that killed most of our vines overnight .... The fields do not produce enough to keep alive a family of six people...."

She hesitated and turned her ivory face towards the window as if she were looking for inspiration to find more trouble to add to the list, but all that came from our fruit-orchard was the joyous twittering of birds. I had a funny feeling in my stomach and an oppression in my chest as if for lack of air. I longed for the open sky and thought of our two goats.... I wished I were at the *spiazzoi* running with the goat herd, but the voice of Siora Erminia drew me back to the stage of our theater.

Siora Erminia's eyes focused suddenly on Emma and I noticed that Emma's lips were trembling.

"Here is where Emma can help us," she finally burst out with a sense of relief as if she had freed herself of an unwelcome burden. I was now all ears and so was Maria who sat in her chair, her face impassible, her hands crossed in her lap.

Emma was the lamb in the family, the person to whom each of us could turn for whatever we wanted her to do. And she would do it, and sacrifice herself no matter the cost, never asking for anything for herself. She had in her own way a beautiful face especially when she smiled, which she did very rarely. But she was afraid of her own shadow. How could Emma help us out of trouble, if Mare who could lead an army into war could not do it? Perhaps by praying like Pare.

Maria and I looked at each other. We knew we were thinking the very same thing. Maria confessed to me later that she thought Siora Erminia had arranged Emma to marry a very rich, very old man. And Maria wished she had been in Emma's place.

"As you know," Siora Erminia continued while handling her rosary as if she were reciting her beads, "our Saintly Bishop, God bless his soul, is such a conscientious shepherd of his big flock not only for the sake of God, but also of our dear Emperor in Vienna, that he and his collaborators can hardly sleep at night...."

Having made sure that we all agreed on this important point, she courageously brought her boat into the harbor.

§ § §

"Among the Bishop's collaborators the saintliest and the most precious is Monsignor Bertolini.... You could not think of anyone more devoted to the Bishop, more trusted, more needed in these difficult days... But this most worthy Monsignor is old and sick. He needs physical and moral support.... He needs someone else, besides his housekeeper — a very experienced and worthy woman to be sure, but old herself.... The Monsignor in question is the Dean of the *Cathedral of Trento*...."

She spelled these last words slowly to impress us, but the only one who seemed to be impressed was Mare. Emma's hands were trembling. I felt as if we were in a carriage driven by Siora Erminia which was skirting the brim of a precipice. I heard the boys making a loud noise in the kitchen as if they were having a fight. And I trembled for the just punishment they would later get from Mare.

Finally, Siora Erminia with an energetic, sudden jerk of the reins led our carriage to safe ground.

"What we need is the proper occasion to introduce Emma to Monsignor Bertolini. And here is where God and your saintly father, God bless his soul, came to our help. My sister Clementina's daughter, Baroness Cornelia Taxis is engaged to marry the nobleman Tullio de Panizza Inama von Brunnenwald, a most faithful servant of the Church. During the festivities marking their marriage, which will gather in our home the best of Trento and the world around us, I plan to make sure that our dear Emma is not only properly introduced to Monsignor but I shall see to it that her excellent qualities are properly appreciated and she will happily live from now on not in any old house in Trento but in the splendid palace adjacent to the ancient famous cathedral so important in the history of our church. Live there and send home the money which is needed for the survival of the family."

As she mentioned the marriage, she turned to her sister the Baroness. I could swear that there were tears in Siora Erminia's steel blue eyes, whereas the Baroness blushed as happy as she could be and looked at us to make sure we were sharing her joy.

§   §   §

That was it. Emma had to leave us, Emma who, after Virginia's death held us together by doing for us the most humble services, to whom we turned for help and support when we needed it. Emma would move into another world, the world of Trento, which for us then was farther than the moon.

§   §   §

What Siora Erminia was arranging for us was the first and most painful break in the family structure. So painful it made us all sick to our stomach for many days. We had so far lived a protected life in our village. Our home was our world. Our mother our Queen. The food we ate came mostly from our fields no matter how poor they were. Now Emma's departure opened the gates to a world we all feared for reasons we did not understand....

After a few days of silence, Emma was resigned to go. Her departure was like death. We accompanied her one morning to the stage coach. Damiano carried her small carpet-bag containing one dress, two aprons and some underwear.

Before she left home, she knelt in the *Stua* near the big bed to get Mare's blessings. Mare's face was as white as Siora Erminia's. "God be with you," Mare said.

§ § §

Siora Erminia kept her word. Emma was received with open arms by old Monsignor Bertolini, who would have liked to see gentle, sixteen year-old Emma working near him. But the old house-stewardess, who had been around for forty years, jealous of the newcomer, made sure she was confined to the backrooms with ironing and storing laundry, and never missed an occasion to reproach her for being a barbarian fallen on civilized Trento from the dark valleys.

Siora Erminia on the other hand, far from giving up the fort under siege, moved to an open attack and convinced Monsignor Bertolini to have Maria join Emma in Trento. Maria's departure was not sad at all. We knew Maria would console Emma who was missed at home terribly. Besides, Maria had been longing for some time to break not from the family but from the sacrifices imposed by our poverty on all of us. What she disliked most was working in the fields. Maria was a happy soul who liked to laugh, dance and enjoy herself in every possible way.

News from the two together in Trento made us all happy. Maria made Monsignor laugh so much with stories from the family and the village — including the story of Siora Erminia's visit in the 'room in the middle' — that he invited Mare to Trento for her birthday with me and Damiano. Mare's birthday coincided with the feast of St. Joseph on March 19.

§ § §

Damiano was fifteen and I was twelve when, holding Mare's hand, we boarded the stage coach that took us down the Val di Non to the confluence of the Noce with the Adige which is a real river not a wild torrent like the Noce. The train was a horrible experience. It moved incredibly fast, huffing and puffing a dark acrid smoke in our eyes.

"Get your head in from the window!" Mare screamed to Damiano and people looked at her in disdain because Damiano acted as if he didn't hear her. Now that he was away from the village he felt free to act as he wanted. Damiano was dumb. In school he never spoke, but at home he used words he would have never said, had Pare been alive. In spite of it all, I liked him.

§ § §

Emma was waiting for us on top of the stairs of the Bishop's palace where she lived: "Clean your shoes and watch out for the house stewardess," she told us, but we knew how to act because we had been warned. And Damiano was, fortunately for us, quite scared at the newness of the place.

"She wants to get rid of both of us, me and Maria, because she is jealous," Emma told us in one breath, "but the Monsignor likes us. He'll like you too, but you must speak Italian not *noneso* and kneel when you see him and kiss his ring."

We promised Emma to do what she said, though Damiano couldn't say anything in Italian.

§ § §

As soon as we entered the room and saw the Monsignor, I ran to him and fell on my knees and grabbed the Monsignor's right hand. I saw a golden ring with a big stone on his little finger and kissed that stone hard and said '*Bondì*' which means 'Good day.' Damiano stumbled and fell. It was awful. But the Monsignor got up from his red velvet armchair. He was dressed in a long black silk robe, topped with a red cape and a bit of a red hat. He laughed heartily and took my hand and led me to Damiano and we both got him back on his feet. I was embarrassed for Damiano who had tears in his eyes. He looked miserable because he felt he had failed the test and Emma and Maria would punish him. Mare stood silent at a distance. We all forgot about her.

Monsignor was short and skinny, with no beard and no moustache. I could hardly believe he was a Monsignor. He was a friend, somebody I could talk to and with whom I could laugh. We sat with him for a long while and he asked me what I liked best. I said goats, and I asked him, and he said he also liked goats. He smiled. And there was silence. Then we talked at length about goats and pastures and fields and flowers and how I liked to set flowers in vases after I had swept the house clean. We had a marvelous time together before he had to go back to work with the Bishop. Then he called Emma, and all of us, Mare and Damiano and me and Emma and Maria, had dinner in the kitchen with chicken and eggs and noodles and even a cake, something we don't eat at home, not even on Easter.

§ § §

That day in Trento was full of surprises. We saw from the windows of the living room the *ciode* that is the *cucciarecazzote*, the poor women who came in from Italy. They would all gather in the square in front of the Cathedral while the ladies of Trento would bargain for them to get them as housecleaners. That's what Maria explained to us. She was proud of being in the Bishop's palace and we all were too. Maria looked like a different sister from what she was in Tajo. She wore a starched white blouse and a full black skirt and acted as if she was Monsignor's stewardess. She stood behind us, her hands on her hips. We were lucky, she said, not to be Italian. Look at those children down there under the linden trees, hanging on to their mother's skirt, crying. Their mothers sell themselves for a day's work because they are so hopelessly poor. You couldn't see anything like this in our villages.

§ § §

A few days later, Mare left with Damiano and I remained behind in Trento at the Monsignor's Palace without anybody telling me why. The morning after Mare's departure, Maria washed me from head to foot, combed my hair, and dressed me in a blue skirt and a white blouse. All this before breakfast. Then I was led to the *tinello* where I found, sitting around the table, the Monsignor of Santa Maria and Maestra Garelli.

He was a plump priest dressed more or less like our Monsignor. She was all in black, a black hat topping her outfit, a hat that looked like a bird's nest. I couldn't get over that hat and how ugly she was as I went through additions and subtractions, divisions and multiplications. They made me also write a few lines in Italian. It was fun and I enjoyed it.

Later in the day Maria came to get me in Emma's laundry room. She was overjoyed. "You passed the exam!" she shouted in my ear, as if I were deaf, and lifted me in her arms and kissed me and embraced me. I had never been embraced like that in my life. From that day on I always liked to take exams.

"Now," Maria said, "what we need is Mare's permission." "For what?" I asked.

"Of course — for you to stay in Trento to study to be a teacher. In four years you can be a *teacher*! Unbelievable!"

I was dumfounded. A teacher? All the teachers I had seen so far were old and ugly. They must have a miserable life. As I sat alone in Emma's back room looking out of the window, all I could see was a small slice of blue sky not bigger than a handkerchief. I thought of my goats running free at the *spiazzoi* and felt no end miserable. I cried desperately that night cuddled in Emma's arms. But why cry about it? I felt sure Mare would say 'no, I want my daughter back with me in the village.'

Mare's answer took quite a while to come. I was told later that she went to the parish priest for advice and to the old teacher, the sister of the one who taught me, who was also my godmother. They both knew only too well what Mare had to go through in order to save the house from the creditors a few weeks after my birth. She had to find thousands of Kronen! And she had found them, God knows how. Why should she now go through four years of hard sacrifice for a daughter who should be her helper in the fields and at home?

"If you were the Marini," they both said, "we would say yes, go ahead, but for you, poor woman, it is not a good speculation. Do not give in to temptation. Get that child to help you survive. Get her to work like her sisters to support the family!"

§ § §

Monsignor Bertolini turned Mare's 'No' into a 'Yes'. He would pay for my expenses through the four years. Emma and Maria announced to me that I would leave Trento shortly to spend the summer with Monsignor in the country at Romagnano to get ready for my future schooling….

§   §   §

From May 1901 on, no matter where I was and with whom, my life was spent mainly on books, pencil in hand. I had to make it, and well. I knew there was no way out for me or the family. Not only our honor but our very life was at stake.

As long as I lived with Monsignor, my life was easy. I got up every morning at five to review my homework. At eight punctually Miss Berenice Ecker would show up in the Monsignor's *tinello*, a young woman all smiles and jokes who didn't look like a teacher at all. I had by that time already attended the Mass celebrated by Monsignor and drank some chicory coffee in the kitchen with my two elder sisters.

Maestra Ecker taught me more use of numbers and better writing. She taught me also two subjects I would love for life: the history of the people of the world and all about the places where they lived, that is geography. In September, I was officially told by Monsignor that I had "brilliantly passed my admission exam to the *Magistrali* (Teachers Junior College)." He kissed me on the forehead and laughed when I told him I did not notice I had taken an exam. Next time he should tell me ahead of time.

§   §   §

Monsignor and I got along so well together I felt as if he had always been part of my life, like Mare and Pare and my woods and my goats, although my life in Trento ran on a radically different track than life in Tajo. The old gentleman took me on walks around the city, and while we walked slowly, with him leaning on my arm, he would tell me stories about this or that building. Then the building would come to life for me inhabited by people who had little in common with the people of today.

The stories that impressed me most and made me view the city of Trento as unique in the world, were those about the Cathedral itself. Bishops of Trento had been for centuries powerful Princes of the Church and of the Empire. At one point they ruled as the supreme authority over the whole region of Trento and Bozen. At times, it looked as if they were more powerful than Popes. Popes — Monsignor said in a matter of fact way – did not always live according to the life of the Gospel, helping the poor and warning the rich. Once, four hundred or more years ago, a monk in Germany called Luther dared to denounce the mode of behavior of the Court of Rome. Poor people followed him all over, even in my valley, and a war started between him and the Pope. Soon Christians killed each other by burning the 'protesters', that is Luther's followers, in the midst of the public squares. Finally, the Pope decided to gather his wisest men, the Cardinals, to see if they could find a way of stopping the war among Christians and save of the old Church what could be saved. He chose the Cathedral of Trento way up in the North, that is close to Germany, as the place for a Council. The discussion went on and off for thirty years with more and more people coming from Rome, so that some of the Tridentine families today, like the Alberti and the Manci and the Ciani claimed to be descendants of the Italians who came up to Trento almost five hundred years ago. They have titles like Barons and Counts because they can trace the history of their families back to the Council of Trento in the year 1530. A plague, however, put an end to the meetings. Monsignor showed me a big painting of the results of that plague with all the cardinals running away from the Cathedral. When the Cardinals met again they found a solution to the problem: it stopped the war but left the Christian world cut in two, with much killing going on even after the Council closed.

I would have liked to hear more about that 'Council' as he called it and the unhappy solution to the problem, but Monsignor didn't want to go any further, and I didn't dare ask Maestra Eckart about it, because her main concern was with the Romans and the Greeks who lived long before Luther. The one time I mentioned to her the name "Luther" she looked at me in dismay and asked me where did I ever hear *that* name. I didn't say from Monsignor because I did not want to create trouble for him. I had learned that Trento now was the City of the Popes and Luther had no place in it.

Monsignor liked to spend time with me inside the Cathedral, not to pray, which he thought should be done in private, but to show me how the adornments of the church, like the light balconies, contributed with their beauty to uplift our spirit. He also spent time examining paintings with me, pointing out to me the harmony and contrast of colors and styles as he put it. Once he talked about the body of the dead Christ lying on Mary's lap and talked about it as if it were the body of a common man. It made me think of Pare's body when I had washed it with Mare to prepare it for burial. I told him so and he said yes, Jesus was a man like Pare even if he was the Son of God. Then he added: "We choose to believe by faith things that are unbelievable."

I did not go and didn't miss going home for many months, not even for Christmas. Midnight Mass in the Cathedral of Trento was the most incredible event I ever attended, incredible for others not for me. When, with my own eyes, I saw the Bishop celebrating the Mass, cloaked in crimson and gold, with a golden tiara on his head, leaning on a long scepter like an Emperor, with my Monsignor at his side and all the other Monsignors and priests surrounding him, I *believed* the Cathedral was indeed Paradise. I told Monsignor next morning I did not need Faith to believe in Paradise after that experience. He told me my Faith made his Christmas. Then he added, laughing, that I was *lucky*. I didn't know what he meant by that, but I did not confide with Emma and Maria, because I was afraid they wouldn't understand anything about Faith. I was the only one in the family who knew about it. And decided to keep it a secret.

I was so happy to be *lucky* that working on my homework seemed a joke. I loved my work, every bit of it, but mostly drawing. If I had been made to choose I would have painted all day long. Painting was for me what praying was for Pare.

§ § §

One morning early in February of 1903 Maria interrupted me in my writing exercises. She sat near my desk with a radiant expression in her face:

"Monsignor called me yesterday," she announced, "and told me bluntly that tomorrow he will finalize his written Will and sign it. He wants to make sure that you have a chance to complete your studies in Trento. He knows that Mare cannot support you. He promised her he would. He is going to keep his promise...."

Then she embraced me with her eyes shining like stars: "I am sure he doesn't do that out of duty, as an obligation. He told me flatly that you are much more deserving than he thought. He said there is nothing he enjoys more than talking to you. He prays God, he said, to be allowed to live long enough to see you moving on year after year, until someday you'll be the best teacher in the world."

While living near Monsignor during the past months I had never thought of my 'future.' I believed in the kind of world he had opened for me. What Maria said hurt me deeply. She made me aware that Monsignor could be taken away from me like Virginia and Pare. The work in school that day became suddenly a heavy burden to carry. It snowed all day. The palace was bitterly cold except for the kitchen and the *tinello*. I did not see Monsignor that evening. He spent all day working with the Bishop until late at night.

Next morning at five, when I moved with my candle to the kitchen, Emma was sitting near the table, her head hidden in her hands. She was sobbing. When she heard me approaching she got up and took me in her arms. Monsignor had died of a stroke during the night. Maria joined us without tears, disheveled and pale: "He did not make it to sign the will," she said. "He was a Saint. He'll pray for us in Heaven, like Virginia and Pare. But we are, all three of us, left in the hands of that *Witch*. Yesterday, when he expressed his desire to sign the Will, she told him there was always time to do that...."

The name of the house-stewardess was Caterina, but Maria never called her by name. I did not know how Maria could discover what was said and done behind closed doors.

Within one month the household of Monsignor Bertolini was dismantled. He had no family and no will. Emma, Maria and I were left to fare on our own.

§ § §

"One thing is sure," Maria declared the day after Monsignor's death, standing straight in front of Emma and me, her hands on her hips. "We are not going back to the village." She took our silence for consent and added: "And we shall not join the poor Italian women either on Sunday morning in front of the Cathedral!"

Since she felt sure that on this point we agreed, she concluded with a firm voice that admitted no discussion: "And we shall not write to Mare until we have a decent address, which means we make enough money to live decently."

From that moment on, Maria became our point of reference.

The first, most painful blow for us was to accept to separate and thus renounce to the daily, almost hourly comfort of each other's presence. Siora Erminia came to our help, though she was now in trouble herself because of her nephews, Sior Augusto's children. Emma was housed as a seamstress by Mrs. Vedovelli, a friend of Siora Erminia. I found temporary shelter in the house of a distant cousin. Maria wriggled her way into the household of one of the most powerful families of Trento, the Counts Alberti. Within their palace she climbed rather rapidly from kitchen to laundry room, to chambermaid of the countess, to waitress at the table, until, within a relatively short time, she had become the head stewardess of the whole Alberti household — a palace in the city, a villa in the country — with a heavy set of keys swinging from her waist.

"That witch would die of envy seeing me here!" Maria whispered to Emma and me as she received us in her new kingdom, hinting to old Caterina, Monsignor's stewardess. She laughed, but I felt a pang in my heart. I missed Monsignor. I had felt him close to me for the last time during the funeral given to him by the Bishop. The Cathedral had never been so imposing, the music so enchanting. Where was he now? Did it really matter where I lived from now on, if his world had vanished with him? Maria gave me a harsh look: "As for you," she said, looking straight into my eyes, "you had better straighten yourself out. You had it too easy until now...."

Our meeting point was now a backroom in the Alberti Palace which was assigned to Maria as the administrator of the household.

She had made sure Mare knew her daughters lived now in a palace with a painted façade.

Emma and Maria helped me financially to survive the rest of the year in school after Monsignor's death. Emma sent her entire salary to Mare and Maria most of hers. She made no mystery that she wanted to set aside some money for herself, for her dowry, she said, though she planned to marry a rich old man who did not ask for a dowry. By the time I went back to the village for the summer after Monsignor's death, I knew that from now on if I wanted to go back to the city and complete my studies I had to fare on my own. I had just turned fourteen.

Never for a moment did I entertain the doubt that I could give up school. I had a serious obligation to go through it successfully not only towards Mare, who was proud of me beyond words, and my two sisters, but mostly towards my dear dead, Virginia, Pare, and Monsignor, all three of whom, I strongly believed, supported my efforts from wherever they were. So that very first summer in Tajo I organized a group of girls from the Val di Non who studied in Trento and, with Maria's invaluable help, we found an old, very pious woman who was willing to house us in her ample loft. We would get food from our families in the valley, cook by ourselves, and pay a little extra for the *paion*, a kind of sack filled with dry corn leaves, on which we slept, besides of course the wood we used for cooking. We kept the pious lady's house spotlessly clean.

Studying was hard for me at first because I had lost Monsignor and the exciting new world he had opened to my mind and soul with the security of his home and mostly with his friendship. Gone forever was also the world I had given up in order to live in Trento: the meadows, the forests, the open sky, Mare's warm kitchen during the cold winter evenings, and Mare's strong arms, the trust I used to have in her that gave me such security. When despair and loneliness overwhelmed me at night I buried my face in the rough *paion* and cried silently so as not disturb my companions who were as badly off as I was. Almost always I was so tired I soon fell asleep. I never turned for comfort to Maria who would have made fun of me for 'being a sissy' nor to Emma who seemed now more lost than ever. Surviving, I guess, took most of my energy.

§ § §

The pious woman who housed us at first was old, rude, and as cold as a fish. Standing erect as if she had swallowed a broom stick, she would have liked to mold us girls in her image and likeness. Every morning we had to attend with her the early mass at six in the morning, which would had been for us the best time for studying.

"God comes first," she stated as she slammed the door of the house behind us leading us to church. The day, thank God, was for school. We had to be home by sunset so as to clean her house before dinner. What bothered us girls most was the feeling that what gave our host the greatest satisfaction was to deprive us of time for studying, which for her was a distraction from praying and from purely manual work. A perverse instinct spurred her to deprive us gratuitously from the minimal relief from the harshness of life. She saw us as miserably poor girls from the barbarian valleys, entrusted to her by our families to work and pray God. The world around us, she said, was full of temptations. Thank God for the temptations, we laughed among ourselves when, on our way home from school, we began unconsciously to enjoy the city itself. During the cold wintry months Trento came to life with Carnival. The joyous toot of the first cars made boys and girls run screaming with excitement, while ladies dressed up for church or for shopping or for the theatre, some arm in arm with black dressed gentlemen, paraded laughing on the slippery streets, balancing their beautiful hats on their heads, their hands sunk in their thick fur muffs. The city itself was for us theater at its best. And then there was Maria.

"I'll get you to take part in the *far la volta al Sass*," Maria announced one beautiful day at the closing of Carnival. She had sworn to herself she would give a lesson to our landlady. She took us to the countess' wardrobe, dressed us up, found masks for us. And there we were, all six of us girls, twirling fast in our dance within the inner of two concentric circles, with the boys on the outside. We went on laughing and dancing and singing even after sunset. Maria herself had us all washed and cleaned before taking us back to the old lady who was furious. "What would God say?" she kept on screaming. We didn't answer, but next morning in school we had just as much fun as the day before in putting together a letter addressed to her as

"Our Saintly Rose Bud." Though it was unsigned, we waited to mail it until the last day of the academic year. We couldn't afford losing the roof over our head.

In the fourth and final year the work in school was so hard and exacting we decided to change residence and split into small groups. Three of us who were poorer than the others found the only home we could afford in the dark but spacious den of the cathedral's bell-ringer, a hunchback who worked as a shoemaker. In the back of the den lay the bell-ringer's invalid sister, her eyes closed as if she was dead. The three of us slept around her. The den, carved within the walls of the old cathedral, was dimly lit from a door on a blind alley so narrow that the sun never reached it. Lack of daylight forced us to study always with candles, which, we soon discovered, added considerably to our monthly expense. Four months a year the den was freezing cold. I did my homework leaning on the shoemaker's desk, wrapped tight in a heavy blanket, as close as possible to the modest fire our host lit in the chimney. That fire allowed the poor man to work as a blacksmith in his spare time. When we got up in the early morning during the winter months we broke the ice in the basin with a stick to wash our faces. But none of us three girls complained. The old man was for us the source of such fun that we were happy to share with him what he pompously called his 'residence.' When, late at night, we would eat together our boiled potatoes and herrings on his shoemaker's desk, he would entertain us with the 'sins' of the rich and of the nobility of Trento which he claimed he had overheard from a hole in the walls of his den that communicated directly with the Bishop's confessional. His stories, which made us laugh hysterically, counterbalanced the difficulties of our daily life. I never slept as soundly and peacefully as in that den, grateful to my beloved dead in Heaven that the Cathedral, under whose noble and generous auspices I had begun my life in Trento, had offered me in the end the best possible chance to see it from a hole in its walls. At times, in that dark den I felt as free as in Tajo's woods.

§ § §

What kept the three of us walking happily to school in the morning was seeing the light at the end of the tunnel, that is graduation. Besides, some of the subjects I studied were absolutely fascinating for me. Arithmetic had turned into algebra and geometry, which I adored. Pedagogy into history of ideas. We also learned poems that magically transformed the world around us and during art I could paint to my heart's content. I was in peace with myself and with the world. I was happy because I did what I wanted to do, Monsignor would have said.

In June 1907, I approached the final examination in full awareness that it was a test for which I had studied during the previous four years. I had studied so hard and had enjoyed so much what I had to learn, that I faced the final exam without any apprehension. I wasn't at all surprised that I passed with excellent grades.

§ § §

Emma, who was now working in the laundry room of the Counts Alberti, cried silently for joy, her tears falling on the beautiful blouse that she was ironing. Maria lifted me in her robust arms laughing and crying, and boasted aloud about me to the Countess and her family.

Count Edoardo Alberti called me the very day of graduation to remind me of my responsibilities as a teacher in the public schools of the Trentino. His sermon focused mainly on my 'national' obligations. Was I aware that Trento and the Trentino were rightly claimed by Italy, that we were actually *Italians,* and sooner or later we had to fight to be recognized as such? Some courageous Trentini were dying now for the 'Cause:' the "Cause," he explained, was Italy and Liberal Thinking. I knew from Monsignor that Count Alberti belonged to the liberal party and was strongly pro-Italian.

While he spoke, boys from the valley, new recruits in the Austrian army, paraded in front of the Alberti Palace singing at the top of their lungs not an Italian but an Alpine song in their native language. I knew those boys had never seen Rome or ever dreamed about it. I thought of my village where people spoke *noneso,* not Italian, of Mare and of the village women happily chatting away in *noneso* while they washed at the public fountain. An overwhelming wave of happiness surged in my heart at the thought that I was about to leave Trento forever. While the Count was speaking close to an open window of his beautiful palace, it dawned upon me suddenly that there was something about the politics and the religion of Trento that I could not understand or accept. It was as if Count Alberti spoke a language foreign to me. Yet, I liked him and thanked him for having been allowed to spend four years in his city. But now I had to leave, I said. And I meant it.

Before dismissing me, the Count gave me as a gift a beautiful antique painting of a Madonna and Child. As I commented on the harmony of colors he smiled, pleased. I thought for a moment I saw Monsignor standing behind him and my eyes filled with tears. Evidently touched, he got up and shook my hand. "Brava!" he said "Lucky pupils! You'll be the best teacher in the Trentino." His Madonna still hangs over my bed.

# CHAPTER 3

## The Devil

Mare was at the stage coach in Tajo waiting for me. She had grown old during my absence and had lost all of her teeth except one, a front tooth which danced in her mouth when she spoke. I felt sick to my heart seeing her like that, but she was out of herself for joy. She held me in her arms as if she had reacquired a precious possession. Then she stated with her usual strong voice: "I'll accompany you to your new assignment and help you settle down." I respectfully rejected her offer. I wanted to face my new responsibilities on my own. She understood and did not insist.

§ § §

My assignment was Segno, a village 5 km from Tajo. One of my obligations as a teacher was to live in the village. And here my troubles started.

Maestra Tarter, the senior teacher who had instructed generations of villagers, was quite a woman. She exacted from everybody a respect mixed with fear, not only because she was well prepared, gifted, experienced and well read, but also because she was a spirited woman who seemed to possess an extra dimension besides the academic one.

Everyone in Segno was aware that, at night, Maestra Tarter sat for hours at her desk, writing long letters to her son Teofilo who lived somewhere in America and was well known there as the leader of his church choir. Every person in Segno admired Teofilo for his extraordinary qualities, especially after the visit to Segno of the American parish priest himself who was received with the honors due the Bishop of Trento. There were other habits of Maestra Tarter of which the village was only partially aware. Since I lived at first in a room over her apartment, I was given the chance early on of becoming acquainted with her strange behavior. For instance, she used desiccated human bones, including skulls, as ornaments along the stairs that led from her apartment to my room. These were interspersed with geraniums and other flowers. She kept in her kitchen three big copper vats of aquavit, spiced with clover and real roasted coffee — a rarity in our country —, which she openly sipped to her heart's content in the evening after church, during her sessions with Teofilo. I took in everything, postponing all judgments, as Mare had taught me.

Maestra Tarter made me understand clearly upon my arrival that the worse thing I could do, given who I was — the daughter of a poor family who owned only two goats, a teacher with a smattering of education in the capital city of Trento, for which she had no respect because students there were 'socialists' which meant friends of the devil —, was to interfere with what she considered her own field of action as a Teacher who had learned from lifelong experience. As the Senior Teacher in Segno she considered it her duty and privilege to lead the rosary every night in church — a task which she performed with a hoarse voice before her letter-writing to Teofilo — and to be present at *every* religious function taking place on Sunday and holidays. I attended all church functions, sitting in the back in silence. But that was evidently not enough.

After a few days in Segno, it became clear to me that the village identified Maestra Tarter with an extra dimension of the church, more spiritistic than spiritual. Some said she could cure the sick and even resuscitate the dead. I decided that for my own good I should refrain from minimally contesting public opinion.

Soon after my arrival I discovered that Maestra Tarter had opposed my assignment to Segno, especially after the information she had obtained about me from her secret agents in Trento: I had been moved from Tajo, fief of the untrustworthy Sior Augusto Panizza — liberal, atheist, author of a book against the witches of the Trentino — to Trento, as a protegée of an equally untrustworthy, although differently so, Monsignor Bertolini. Finally, I had been assigned to Segno as a protegée of Count Alberti. Count Alberti was by far a worse character in her world than either Sior Augusto Panizza or Monsignor Bertolini because he was an enemy of our Emperor and was openly friendly with the atheists and the Italians, who for her were one with the Devil. To make things worse for me, shortly before my arrival, the Valley Inspector, Mr. Paisan, had dared to openly express criticism of Maestra Tarter before the village inspector, Mr. Fiorenzo, a squat stocky peasant who made fun of her in public. She felt sure I was part of the plot against her.

Taking all the above in due consideration, I decided that the safest road for me to follow was what Mare had suggested to us children in case we met a bear in the forest: to lie low until I had succeeded in reassuring her of my intentions not to hurt her.

My first preoccupation upon my arrival was where to live. I was told I would receive the rich lodging bonus of 100 Kronen, part of which I planned to give to Mare in Tajo, if I could enjoy public housing. Yet, the walls of the two-storey, recently built 'public' house assigned to Maestra Tarter and myself by the mayor were still so wet that clouds of minuscule insects swarmed inside the fresh construction. Although the priest, called by Maestra Tarter, repeatedly inundated the rooms with holy water, the insects persisted. Thus Maestra Tarter and I agreed to renounce to public quarters for the time being and I was ordered to move from my temporary room over Maestra Tarter's apartment to an isolated little house outside the village near the big woods that separate one village from another.

From my very first day in Segno, a Monday in September 1907, I enjoyed teaching enormously. The children loved me and truly trusted me, as they showed me on one occasion: during a picnic in the woods one day, while we were peacefully eating, a big bear came close to us. "Lie quiet on the ground!" — I told the children — "bears do not hurt people who do not hurt them." The children followed my advice. The bear came by, ate some of the food and disappeared in the forest. From that moment on, my pupils became my best friends as were their parents and the priest and the mayor and the goats and the cows in the village.

Besides silently attending every function in church, I taught catechism with joy not only in the village but in the villages up the mountain as well.

It was on a golden October afternoon, during one of my long walks through woods and meadows leading to the village of Tora, where I taught catechism, that suddenly, while crossing a meadow which reminded me of the 'spiazzoi' where as a child I pastured my goats, I thought of Sior Gino.

While in Trento, purely by chance, during one of my Sunday visits to Maria at the Albertis, I was shocked to hear the details of Sior Gino's story which had puzzled me since the evening I had overheard Siora Erminia confiding it as a secret to Mare on our *pont*. The cause of Sior Gino's banishment from his family was a woman, a harlot of some kind whom he had brought home from Vienna where he studied. When Sior Augusto had announced one evening to Gino that he had been chosen to be the lucky husband of his cousin, the Baroness Cornelia Taxis, Gino gently apologized and explained to his father that he was already engaged to marry. The woman, whose name was — the chambermaid said — Flora, a foreign prostitute, was expecting. Sior Augusto, locked for hours in his office with his son, argued with all the wit for which he was famous in favor of a reasonable solution to the impasse which would ruin the family's reputation. He offered to pay the 'woman' a good sum, enough to support her with her child for the rest of her life. He reasoned, begged, cajoled, screamed, but to no avail. Sior Gino proved to be just as clever a lawyer for his cause as his father. He had made up his mind. He was going to marry Flora! It was in consequence of his most stubborn disregard for the honor of his family that Sior Gino was disinherited.

The chambermaid of Countess' Alberti had told me the story in all details, with evident complacency, sitting on the Countess's bed. To my dismay, her judgment in the end fell hard on Sior Gino. I wished she hadn't taken me as her audience. I was dismayed. Why should the people of Trento be so harsh on him?

§ § §

"Everybody in Trento agreed," the chambermaid stated with open satisfaction, "that Sior Gino's last resort was to leave the civilized world, that is Europe, forever, and sail beyond the Rock of Gibraltar, — to disappear in America. With his actions he had dishonored his family and his city. The only problem was the fare for the vessel that would take him across the Ocean. That's where the husband of Clodia, Sior Gino's sister came to be useful. The lawyer Beppe Cappelletti, a member of an old family, and a partner in Sior Augusto's firm and the most loyal friend of Sior Gino, was grateful to Sior Gino for having convinced his sister Clodia, some years before, to leave the nunnery — where she had been confined by her aunt, Siora Erminia, — and marry him, a wealthy lawyer twice her age. Avvocato Cappelletti paid for the boat to take Gino to America, that is forever away from us. Some say it was his mother, Siora Maria, who paid, because she adored him. That was back in 1898. But we don't forget."

As I listened, sitting on a stool while the maid made the countess's bed, I imagined the Rock of Gibraltar being one of our own impassable mountains that separate us from Italy and from the sea. Where was Sior Gino now?, I thought with sudden apprehension, as, on that crystal clear October day of 1907, I was crossing the meadows on my way to teaching catechism to the children of Tora. Monsignor surfaced in my mind, one with Sior Gino who was now lost beyond the Atlantic Ocean in the unknown wilderness of America. Had they known each other, Monsignor and Sior Gino, they would have been friends. But perhaps they were now together. For me, at that time, *Paradise*, the present home of Monsignor, and *America*, the present refuge of the derelict Sior Gino, had something in common. I did not know anything for sure about either. I wished Sior Gino could find the peace I felt sure Monsignor was enjoying. The peace I was now enjoying in Segno.

§   §   §

The days of my own peaceful living in Segno were coming to an end. By the end of November the first snow covered the pines behind my little house and the road that joined it with the village. It was during a night of silent snowing that I was awakened by the harsh noise of chains clattering and creaking just out of my door. I bounced out of my bed and ran to the window. All I could see was the glimpse of a shadow disappearing behind the first bend of the road. I was no end puzzled. Home at Tajo on Sunday, I told Mare about the incident and she decided to come along and sleep with me in Segno. I welcomed her offer.

The night between Sunday and Monday, we were both in bed wide awake, almost waiting for the strange 'noise,' when indeed we were overwhelmed by a much stronger rattling than I had heard the first time. Mare's reaction was to jump up and, stick in hand, open the door and give a lesson to whoever was disturbing our peace. But I held her back. In the morning she returned to Tajo angry at Segno, at me, at everybody except God and her dear dead ones.

"Since you refuse to act," she told me as she left, "you'll suffer the consequences of your inaction!"

On Monday morning nothing unusual happened in church where Maestra Tarter led the rosary as usual with a stentorian voice, but at 8 a.m., I was met at the entrance of my classroom by the parish priest. He stopped me from entering the classroom by holding high a crucifix in front of my face; "Don't get close to it," he warned. "You have been visited by the Devil!"

I was not allowed to teach that day or the day after and the voice spread fast through the Valley that the new teacher in Segno was practicing witchcraft and was visited by the Devil himself. The Bishop sent a priest up to Segno who spent two hours interrogating me about the Devil: had I ever had any contact with him before now in Segno, what form did he choose to take, did I try to defend myself against him. I answered and repeated again and again "I have never seen the Devil in my life!"

§    §    §

But he chose to keep on interrogating without allowing me to say a word in answer, until I could not retain myself from asking him: "Why are you so curious about the Devil?" Then he looked at me as if I was insane, took a wooden crucifix out of a purse he carried with him and suggested, as if he were speaking to a child: "When you go to sleep, hold this Crucifix in your hands under the blankets." I gave that Crucifix later to Mare who didn't want to have anything to do with it and brought it to our parish priest. He laughed and said "I'll bring it back to church where it belongs."

I was at first so overwhelmed, as if an avalanche had buried me, but, as the situation very rapidly worsened and I feared isolation, I decided to move courageously into my classroom. As I did so the children surrounded me with joyous screams "To Hell with the Devil!" We had a good laugh together, but I was still afraid… The next day the Valley Inspector came to Segno to subject me to another interrogation. I then decided to march straight to Town Hall. For my good fortune, the mayor was a liberal thinker. He had carried out his own investigation about my case. He made me sit down near him and showed me the letter Maestra Tarter had written to the civic and religious authorities in Trento, to all except him, accusing me of being a witch and communicating with the Devil.

"A farce," the mayor commented laughing. Then he added seriously: "A farce and a tragedy. The poor woman is insane. I don't know what we can do with her."

Coming home that night, light as a bird, I met the father of one of my students.

"I was out on Saturday night snowplowing," he told me, "and saw with my own eyes Maestra Tarter dragging heavy chains back from your house...." That night Maestra Tarter did not show up in church. When I went to school next day, I found Sior Augusto and Siora Maria in class with my children. They had driven to Segno from near-by Tajo to celebrate my victory over the devil.

In the early spring I accepted the offer of transferal from Segno to Tajo. The community of Segno through its mayor not only apologized to me but offered me tenure if I stayed. I would have stayed because I loved the children, but to be a teacher in Tajo had been, from the very first moment I began my studies in Trento, the highest aim in my life.

# CHAPTER 4

## At Home in Tajo and Cincinnati

In Segno I learned to think of the Devil with compassion. In Tajo I learned to love the world and cross the Ocean with my imagination.

To be accepted as a regular teacher in Tajo was not an easy task. The list of the candidates for the position was carefully scrutinized by the communal council headed by the Academic Inspector. The Council chose and the Inspector approved. The Inspector was Sior Augusto de Panizza. It was he who had established the rules and saw to it, case by case, that they were strictly observed.

The position of teacher in Tajo, however, was also better remunerated and more honored than anywhere else in the Valle di Non. The teachers had a special seat in Church, near the Siori Panizza. At the feast of the Candelera, the Roman 'Lupercalia,' celebrating the Virgin's purification forty days after child-birth, when candles were distributed in the old Church of Santa Maria to the authorities in the village, each of the three teachers received one. When I was a teacher in Tajo, Mare kept that 'sacred candle,' as she called it, with great pride and special care. It was used for people about to die during the administration of the extreme unction.

Shortly after I was nominated Teacher in Tajo, Sior Augusto, in his role as Academic Inspector, invited me to visit him in the main hall of his residence. During a hot afternoon in July, when the whole village dozes in silence and one can hear the crickets chirping from the surrounding fields, I walked up to the Mansion with Mare's blessings, dressed in a black silk skirt and a white cotton embroidered blouse Emma had made for me with material provided by Countess Alberti. They were the graduation present of my two sisters.

*La Sala*, where I was to be received by Sior Augusto, was a wide rectangular room on the main floor of the stone mansion, with a very high ceiling and a tile floor. It was sparsely furnished with antique furniture, antique paintings hanging on the white walls. Flowers in bronze amphoras and crystal vases filled the air with a vague fragrance I can still perceive today in my nostrils. A long rectangular oak table with twelve carved chairs occupied the middle of the room. In between the large windows overlooking a garden there was a wooden bench covered with piles of extravagantly colored silk cushions. Cushions of all colors also covered four armchairs which faced the bench. The color of some of the cushions matched the heavy silk curtains which were partially drawn. Through the half-shut blinds and the open windows a soft breeze carried into the room the smell of recently cut grass.

In a corner of *la Sala* stood, in disharmony with the rest, an easel covered with a white sheet. It was as if the room were the background for a painting, or as if it were the object itself for a painting.

As I entered the hall, I instantly took in the shapes, the colors, the fragrances of the room with pleasure. It was, however, that easel that engaged my full attention. That easel called for a painter.

As a child, I had seen Siora Maria here and there in the village, a kind of constant presence. I had seen her painting the portrait of Pare on the *pont*. What I most vividly remembered was the twinkle in her eyes as she interrupted her painting in the square of Santa Maria to detect with pleasure the effect on our faces of one of her horror stories. I remembered the rustling of her purple silk skirt as she bounced like a child from stone to stone through the bumpy roads of the village; the acrid smoke of her cigar which she lit with a swift stroke of a match miraculously extracted from one of her tiny silk purple shoes. As she smoked at times a long-filtered cigarette, she enjoyed sending long puffs upwards, much to our amazement.

That easel evoked in one instant some of the most exquisitely delightful and hilarious moments of my childhood when, free in mind and body from all duties and constrictions, I lived dreams as reality. Monsignor had tried to explain to me, when I revived those moments for him upon his request, that the freedom from all conventions and the sunny laughter of Siora Maria, whom he knew well and admired, had allowed me then to see, through the harsh factual every-day reality, those flickers of bright light that make life worth living. I did not understand what he meant, but was fascinated, as usual, by his explanation and puzzled by the sigh with which he concluded it.

Sior Augusto cut my daydreaming short. Like Mare, during my absence from the village, he had grown old. (Or was I seeing him with different eyes?) He was less godlike than I remembered him, yet handsome in a way I could not explain to myself. He limped towards me without the support of a cane, shook my hand with one strong shake, as if man to man, and motioned to me to sit down. He sat in front of me on an armchair from which he removed the cushions, and addressed me with a directness that caught me by surprise. Until then I had heard him speaking only in public.

"My sister Erminia, were she still with us, would be proud of you today. I am equally proud and happy, because I know we can fully trust you in carrying out for us the most difficult task befalling this incipient century: the education of our children.

I strongly believe that teaching is an art not a science, that is, one does not become, but one is born a teacher. I heard from Monsignor Bertolini first and recently from Count Alberti, among others, that you are a born Teacher. In school you learned to master the most worthwhile subjects. You learned as a student. The best teachers remain students all of their lives. Now the time has come for you to share what you learned so far with our young citizens. You have to be generous with them and give with joy and enthusiasm. They in turn will give generously to the world of tomorrow."

He continued after a brief pause as if he were talking to himself:

"Unfortunately, today's Schools of Education have defined their subject matter as pedagogy...."

He paused again, then with a broad smile that enlightened his severe face he looked at me straight in the eyes:

"I heard that you don't care for pedagogy. You learned the subject by heart to please the teacher and get a high grade. What you love instead is mathematics and poetry, history and geography. Good for you! I think our children in Tajo are lucky to have you...."

He caressed his white beard with his thin long fingers, like a violinist the cords of his instrument. While searching, I think, for the right approach to an idea difficult to express in words, he turned his handsome head in silence towards the window and then back to me. His eyes were shining as he finally uttered the message he wanted to convey:

"I am doing my best at the Austrian Parliament to see to it that we make the profession of teaching prestigious enough to recruit the best possible teachers. We need young people like you.... My duty as Academic Inspector today is to make you aware of what you already know. You have to uphold not in words but in deeds, that is in substance, the sacred duty of your profession: not only to teach but mainly to *educate* the people of our country, which means not only to teach them how to read and write but to lead them to *think* and to believe in and practice those civic virtues that make civilized life possible. *Il nostro compito e' educare il popolo!*...(Our task to educate the people!)" He pronounced the last words in a mellow, yet strong Italian that sounded like poetry to my ears.

A warm wave of pride overwhelmed me at the thought that he, Sior Augusto himself, was addressing me, "*la Beppina del Pero Moro,*" as one of his collaborators. And I pinched myself: "Hello, *Siora Maestra,* in Tajo!"

"There is nothing I wouldn't do for you," I felt like screaming, but then suddenly, coming from nowhere, the blurred image of Sior Gino appeared behind Sior Augusto and I stared at him speechless.

At that moment a door behind the covered easel opened quietly and with the light fairy-like step I remembered so well Siora Maria danced into the *Sala,* a red rose in her black hair, a bouquet of purple peonies in her hands. The charm was broken. The sun was now shining over a different world as she looked at me with a childish smile:

"I read some place that in some country in the world the peony — in spite of its acrid smell — is considered the queen of flowers. Anyway, I brought you peonies because I love them."

Then, handing me the bouquet, she whispered:

"From a Queen to a Queen... We needed a Queen among our teachers. Is it true you like painting? And you like poetry? And history? ... I didn't mean to interrupt a professional meeting, but I hope this is the first of many visits you pay to us...."

She looked at Sior Augusto as if to mockingly ask him for forgiveness. He laughed. It was the first time in my life I heard Sior Augusto laugh.

"My wife, Baroness Maria Ciani, is a passionate painter, a voracious reader and a perfect companion for a serious old man like me," he said. "She is mainly an outspoken liberal thinker. Her family has spent most of its fortune for the national *cause* in which we both believe, the 'redemption' of our land. She is most fervently Italian... I mean an Italian at heart...."

He reached out for her little hand and brought it to his lips.

§ § §

On June 2, 1910, Sior Augusto died suddenly of a heart attack, one year precisely after our first meeting. His sister, Siora Erminia, had died a few months before my arrival in Tajo.

The funeral for Sior Augusto was a ceremony Tajo remembered as long as one of those present survived. There were, besides the relatives, the representatives of the leading families not only of the Trentino, like the Counts Alberti and Manci and the Barons Ciani, but also politicians and professionals from Austria and Italy especially in the juridical field, and common people from the whole Valle di Non. The church was overflowing with flowers. Sior Augusto's contributions to society were extolled in speech after speech. The most touching tribute came from the village farmers and from the school children. They spoke and acted as if they had lost a father, a leader, a point of reference and support.

I was overwhelmed by the loss of an exceptional man. During my first year of teaching I had had the chance of reaping the fruit of Sior Augusto's unconditional support, based on his beliefs in and loyalty to the young, on the seriousness of his commitment. As for the ceremony of the funeral, no funeral could ever again evoke in me a closeness to the dead and an indescribable sense of the divine as Monsignor's funeral did when, at the climax of the ritual, the choir intoned the ancient hymn "*Tantum ergo sacramentum/ veneremur cernui/ et antiquum documentum novo cedat ritui…,*" an invitation to kneel in veneration of the divine represented in the consecrated host as the body of Christ, an exhortation to replace the old with the new rite. Monsignor had translated the hymn for me into Italian. I loved the words of the hymn as Monsignor recited them, but the day of his funeral it was the divine music that accomplished the miracle. Without being able to explain it to myself, I understood then, or rather felt within me, that our Dead continue to live close to us as part of our most intimate world. That funeral made me believe in "the living dead."

We teachers paid a visit of condolence to the family shortly after the funeral. Siora Maria was surrounded by all of her children — all but one — by their wives and husbands and their children, and her friends, and the friends of the friends. She, however, was not herself, nor did she seem to draw solace from the family surrounding her. As we greeted her, she looked in the distance, out of the windows, towards the woods, almost annoyed at all the human 'noise' around her. And she *was* annoyed, she confessed to me later. One of her sons, Antonio, who physically resembled his father but intellectually and morally did not have much in common with him, was about to celebrate his engagement with Siora Cornelia, the pharmacist's daughters. Siora Maria told me later that she was disturbed by the strident co-presence of life and death, in a moment when she felt overwhelmed by the mystery of death.

After everybody left and the big mansion became again her own home — although only an apartment was assigned to her —, one afternoon in early October she surprised me in school as I was dismissing my students. She took me by the hand like a school friend.

"Let us go home together," she proposed with her childish smile that endeared her so much to me. "I need to breathe again, I need to live…."

We spent that afternoon walking together in the woods that surrounded the mansion and sat near the old spring whence the family got its name 'von Brunnenwald,' a place called *Fontanelle*. We talked about the vines that had just been deprived of the grapes, of the birds that scatter for the night after having chatted together at sunset, of the water of the spring that — I told her — in my childhood I used to follow with my imagination in its running away from us to join brooks and rivers and finally the Ocean.

§ § §

"I wonder," she said suddenly almost to herself, "what Cincinnati is like...."

"Cincinnati? What do you mean?" I reacted in surprise.

I remembered a Roman general called Titus Quintus Cincinnatus, an aristocrat who hated the common people they called 'plebeians.' He had been twice a dictator in Rome, once to free Rome from the threat of two neighboring people, a second time to squash a revolt of the poor. He became famous because after each victory he humbly retired to work his own little field. I told Siora Maria I never cared for him.

"No, no," she laughed, "not that one...," and asked me what I knew about America. She was not surprised by my total ignorance.

"We'll learn about America together," she said as she dug a cigarette from her pocket, adapted it to a filter, and lit it. As she sent with satisfaction puffs of smoke towards the purple sunset, the church bells began to ring. She sensed my anxiety and, foreseeing my embarrassment,

"You must go now," she said, "join your mother in church.... I will see you again another day, I need to see you. I don't know why.... Yes, I know why. Because we are just as happy together in silence as in conversation. With my children and their families it is not the same. They create a 'noise' I resent."

Then, looking at me with a quizzical expression in her eyes, "I am well aware, she said, of what people think of me — that I live without religion, worse, that I am an atheist, an infidel to the Pope and the Emperor.... By explaining to them that I feel closer to God when I look at these pine trees than when I listen to the sermon of the parish priest in church, I would make things worse.... But I love and respect your mother. She is a formidable woman who single-handedly saved her family more than once from disaster. I disagree with her political and religious beliefs but I respect her. Her beliefs are intricately interwoven in the cloth of her life. I admire her for her sturdy coherence. In this case, she must — for your own sake and for the sake of the family — protect your reputation. What will the people of Tajo think of the new teacher spending time with an unorthodox... a sinner like me?..."

Her usual sudden laughter dissipated all bitterness.

I stood at the edge of a flowerbed, frozen in time and space, incapable of moving in any direction, caught between two worlds, two women equally dear to me. I could not free myself from the enchanted garden and could not silence within me the echo of Mare's voice calling me from the church where I was expected to be with her.

With a mischievous smile, Siora Maria got me out of the impasse. She gently took me by the hand and led me to the gate:

"You must go now," she said. "Listen to the bells. This is the second and last call to prayer. I love the sound of those bells. I shall be praying with you and Mare here under the stars."

§ § §

The next day — it was Sunday — after Mass Siora Maria came down from her mansion to our home to visit Mare. The two of them spoke together sitting close to each other on the *pont*, as Mare and Siora Erminia used to do when I was a child who had never seen the world beyond the village. At the end of their long chat I was invited to join them.

"From tomorrow on, when you are free and feel like it, you should spend a few hours of the afternoon with Siora Maria," Mare declared with the pride of a general who has just signed an important official agreement with his enemy counterpart. "Sior Augusto and Siora Erminia will be happy to see you two together...."

Siora Maria smiled with satisfaction. She had promised Mare she would not speak with me of either religion or politics. In Mare's presence from now on she refrained from smoking.

§ § §

From that Sunday on, Siora Maria's tiny black silhouette became a welcome presence for my schoolchildren. If she did not pick me up after classes were over, they would have looked for her up at the mansion, fearing something had happened to her, had I not forbidden them to do so as an interference in her privacy.

My children loved Siora Maria because she entertained them with funny stories to counterbalance, she said, the drudgery of my teaching. I don't know how she managed to get them interested in colors and sounds. "What is the world without painting and music?" she remarked. "All I do is make them aware that they are alive."

Poetry, she told them, is something between painting and music, a magic way of using words. The poet makes you see images through beautiful sounds. And she recited to us by heart Italian poetry, passages from the *Divine Comedy* and of the *Orlando Furioso*.

During the winter there was an interruption in her visits. Her daughters, Clodia and Gemma, insisted she should spend time with them in Clodia's villa in Trento in order, they said, to create a break in her boring life in the village and mainly to become acquainted with her grandchildren.

She left Tajo against her will. She did not have, she insisted, any natural inclination for taking care of grandchildren. "All I do for them, they rightly say, is to distribute candies that smell of tobacco because I keep them in my pocket close to my cigars. Besides, Tajo for me is not boring at all. It is my work place."

§ § §

When the first mild spring breeze melted the snow in the valley and the first snow-drops and violets broke through the still half frozen earth at "Fontanelle," the spring in her woods, there she was again, opening wide the big windows of her mansion in Tajo, this time as free as a lark in the spring singing away her song with the rising sun.

"I carry my husband in my heart, not hidden under my clothes," she explained to me one day laughing again as she used to.

She had given up the conventional 'mourning uniform' — a black dress, black hat with veil — for her normal extravagant silk skirts of the rustling kind, purple or pastel green, pink and blue with matching blouses. "She was not herself in black," remarked a young girl one day," because Siora Maria is made for colors."

As part of the spring 1911, we greeted her tiny colorful silhouette, her head crowned by hair dyed pitch black — with an ointment she herself prepared —, held together by a special wide comb she had bought in Milan, a fresh red rose on her right ear. Heavy coral necklaces and coral ear-rings were as much part of her personality as the tiny silk shoes which I so admired in my childhood.

During the four years we lived close to each other — from 1911to 1914 — I learned from Siora Maria what I could have never learned directly from books, schools, official teachers: a perspective on life that allowed me to harmonize my own world as a farmer's daughter in a small village in the central Alps with the world at large, beyond the mountains that separated us from Italy and the sea. She finally made me discover with her a world beyond the Ocean, beyond the Rock of Gibraltar. That Rock—she declared one evening in a dramatic tone—had done its best for millennia to cut off our old continent from the mysterious world of America. Since we lived in a time of unbelievable technological discoveries, we should soon envisage crossing the Ocean like crossing a wide river. Then she recited to me in her soprano voice some lines from Dante about an old Ulysses who dared to go beyond Gibraltar and miserably drowned with a few old friends in the middle of the Atlantic Ocean. But after Ulysses comes Columbus, Siora Maria added with a mischievous laughter. So, following the road opened by Columbus, we learned a little at the time to courageously look together beyond the kingdom of the setting sun, even beyond the Other Shore of the Atlantic, at a city in the Great Plains called 'Cincinnati' where her Columbus, that is Sior Gino, had established his home.

As the years moved on, I discovered that, after the death of Sior Augusto, Sior Gino progressively dominated Siora Maria's thoughts, her heart, her soul, until, I discovered one day, she was literally devoured inside by an unconquerable longing for him, a desire to embrace him again, to speak and laugh with him, as she had done throughout most of her life. Being an outgoing, hypersensitive woman, she could hardly hide her anxieties from me. Yet she managed for a while with great adroitness to control herself and even if she did not completely hide her pain from me, she made an effort not to make it the main focus of the hours we spent together.

As time moved on, such harmony arose between us that one by one all barriers crumbled and, as she put it, we didn't know anymore who was the teacher and who was the student. We lived so happily together she didn't want to disturb that harmony with her own personal worries. Both of us had the right and the duty to keep her privacy and her independence of action and of thought. After having overcome the first shock of widowhood, Siora Maria declared she would never give up her newly conquered independence. For a woman, she insisted, independence is a question of life or death.

In our conversation she avoided personal issues and categorically rejected with disgust all gossip. Every human being, she strongly believed, no matter how vicious he or she may be, hides a bit of good within himself. No human being should be judged by another human being. An extreme case was the death penalty which she emphatically condemned with arguments taken from Sior Augusto. What she meant, however, was that we should stop short of passing judgment on the actions of our neighbor. She ironically proved her point not only with the Gospel, which she knew like Dante by heart, that is by quoting the parable of Jesus and the adulteress, but by quoting as well Augustine's *Confessions*, a copy of which she kept on her night table. Gossip itself, she insisted, although it may seem like an innocent pastime, can severely damage our neighbor. She would quote the poet Ariosto whose poem I had never read.

§ § §

What we loved to do at first was to walk and talk, but as Siora Maria took up all of her old habits one at a time, she began painting again, and at first, I painted near her. At one point she engaged in serious work on the panels of the doors in her mansion and began drawing and then painting elaborate hunting and mythological scenes. She asked me then to help her in her work by reading aloud from the poems which inspired her subjects: mainly from Ovid's

*Metamorphoses* and Ariosto's *Orlando Furioso*, as well as, of course, from *The Divine Comedy* which, she said, could not have been written without Dante's love for Ovid. She had discovered all of these books, not in the nun's boarding school, for which she had no nostalgia, but on her own, near her mother who was also a painter.

Siora Maria did not pick me up at school anymore, but waited for me at her home, insisting that our meetings should not interfere with our independence. When I showed up one day after a few days of non-previously announced absence, she stopped my apologies short: "Why do you apologize? The road to Hell, they say, is paved with excuses.... You are a free person, free to come and go when you want.... Do not come if not for pleasure."

I would normally sit down near her, book in hand, and begin my reading as she painted. At times, however, she would stop me short. "Aren't you tired of 'great books?' Don't you want us to go back to the novel we liked so much?" (With her I had discovered the world of Russian and French novels.) She returned from her brief visits to Trento or Vicenza in Italy — the home of her family, the Barons Ciani — or sometimes Innsbruck and Vienna loaded with political journals, travel and fashion magazines. She refrained from discussing politics with me, as she never discussed religion, because of the agreement she had made with Mare. We would sit together instead on the colorful cushions of the wooden bench in her *Sala*, magazines scattered all around us, and dream of where we would like to go or how we would look dressed like this or like that. Her curiosity and thirst for life under every form was inexhaustible.

Once I interrupted her in her painting and like a child devoured by curiosity I asked her to tell me her own version of a 'political' anecdote that concerned her. I had heard it when I was fourteen from the old *comare* (gossips), in our *stua*. Everybody knew it in the village: how one day she upset the Austrian police with a joke and was severely reprimanded.

"There is really nothing to it," she declared in a matter of fact tone. "The story is very simple. A gross misinterpretation on the part of our Emperor's police of my motivations in doing what I did. It happened," she smiled, "in 1900, at the dawn of the century. I thought we were entitled to an act of independent thinking on such an auspicious occasion, but the Austrian police has no understanding for independent thinking, at least not the one stationed for the occasion in Tajo. So they totally misinterpreted my action.

It was a beautiful day in September when Prince Eugene, the serene heir to the Austrian Throne, and his wife decided to visit our province. I was told they would actually ride through the main road of the village between the Church and our mansion, not the one where I live now, but, our official residence. Now, in those days — I do not remember exactly when — King Umberto of Italy was atrociously murdered by an anarchist. So I thought — and my husband agreed with me — that in the general rejoicing for the passage of a member of royalty through our village, one person at least could show a sign of mourning for an equally important royal member who had tragically died. I ordered all the windows of our residence shut and a black cloth hung from the central balcony. When I offered the Austrian police this simple explanation, they dryly ordered me to have immediately all windows wide open and a red velvet cloth displayed from the central balcony. Of course I obeyed.... That was it. Nothing more, nothing less." I detected in her relating the story a bitterness I had never noticed before. From that moment on, I refrained from even vaguely touching upon any political subject.

§   §   §

During the summer of 1912, the 'Sior Gino' dimension within the inner world of Siora Maria took such gigantic proportions that, no matter how much she tried, she could not manage to exclude it anymore from the life we happily shared.

"The seeds of roses and peonies growing in Gino's garden in Cincinnati have finally arrived. We can sow them together today, if you don't mind."

She received me one evening proudly exhibiting a package she had just opened. I was more than happy to take care of the 'sowing' for her. She looked too frail to break the ground with a spade. How could I not notice during the months that we lived close to each other that Siora Maria was an old lady, of my mother's age, growing older and weaker by the day under my eyes? How could it escape me that she needed my physical as well as my moral support?

As we watered together the ground over the seeds now peacefully resting in the bosom of the earth in her garden, she whispered to herself, following her thoughts, oblivious, I thought, of my presence:

"... My Gino has been suffering a lot after his wife left him. Yet, in spite of the humiliation and the pain she inflicted on him, he forgave her, when she came back, sick with tuberculosis, and cared for her until she died. He buried her in one of those American cemeteries that have no trees and no flowers, only grass and a stone for each dead with a brief inscription. Now there he is, alone in the evening when he comes back home from the Bank.... At least the roses and the peonies he planted in his garden, upon my suggestion, after she left him, will keep him company...."

§ § §

Perhaps the confession was unintentional. But the ice was broken. While sitting together under the pine-trees of "Fontanelle" the day after the sowing of the American seeds, she invited me to join her in exploring the very special America that now, in 1912, housed such a noble and extraordinary individual as her beloved Gino. Since by the fall of 1912 we had become familiar with Sior Gino's garden and house, we delved with shared enthusiasm from that moment on in the discovery of the city that hosted them.

For the purpose Siora Maria exhibited one after the other the almost daily letters she had received from her son from 1900 on. She read aloud to me excerpts of those letters with pride and emotion in her voice. This proud old lady was at the same time the fiercest custodian of her son's privacy. I could intuit that she was still badly hurt by the gossip that for years had surrounded her son's disappearance. All she wanted now was to do him justice. All she longed for, now that he was alone on the other side of the Ocean, was to live close to him in spirit, almost without his knowing, to share his experiences, to see with his eyes the world that surrounded him stretched wide outside the walls of his house.

Our friendship deepened as, with our imagination, we crossed the Ocean together, excited not only by Sior Gino's letters but also by what we discovered in the rich library of Sior Augusto, and in the library of the Cathedral in Trento, as well as in the Municipal Library of Trento, which Sior Augusto himself had founded. Siora Maria was just as proud of that Library as of Sior Augusto's book which collected all the trials of witches in the Trentino from the seventeenth century to the present, a book she kept near her bed, close to her Dante, her Bible, and her Shakespeare.

§ § §

Unintentionally, however, and almost by chance, in spite of Siora Maria's reticence to discuss her son's personal life, in spite of her jealously hiding details of her son's private life in America before he reached success and peace of mind in Cincinnati, I became aware of her heartbreaking suffering as well as of that of her husband at their son's departure. The pain following Sior Augusto's decision to disinherit his favorite son might have been one of the causes of his death.

As for Sior Gino, I unintentionally discovered that, after a stormy crossing of the Atlantic, he had landed at Ellis island with his wife and a two railroad tickets for Chicago. For some reason he decided to meet life in New York with the $50 he owned. He survived the first months on bread and dry herrings, that is until he found work — or resigned himself to accept whatever work was available — like most poor immigrants, as a longshoreman in the New York Harbor. He also discovered within himself as yet unknown natural gifts which made him the perfect assistant in a zoo — or a circus — to a well-known tamer of rhinoceros. No matter how difficult life was — or perhaps because the kind of life New York offered to him was harsher than he could stand —, he focused all of his attention on learning English. He even wrote up his own little grammar and compiled his own dictionary in which he distinguished literary from popular language. He also had enough good sense to live in what he called 'downtown Manhattan,' the most crowded section of town. He chose for his home the dirty, dark basement of a building on Wall Street. There he met the tamer in the circus and that's how he got his first real job. He did not however stop at that job, although he was making good money. The building where he lived housed a bank or rather more than one bank, a fact which opened new horizons to an immigrant like him who spoke and wrote fluent German, Italian, Spanish, and French and had a degree in law from an Austrian University. Through a doorman he met a banker for whom the doorman bought cigars and newspapers. That doorman gave him the opportunity to carry out himself that important task. As soon as the banker, who spoke German, found out Sior Gino could read and write German better than him — that is literary German — and French and Italian in the bargain, he had him employed as an interpreter in the Bank where he worked.

This happened, of course, after Sior Gino had managed to tame, in addition to the rhinoceros, the language spoken around him. He confessed in a letter to his mother that learning English from German was a joke. Within four months of his arrival he spoke and wrote English fluently. In letter after letter he celebrated the joy of learning English and the beauty of the language, while I at least expected him to give a few details about the rhinoceros of the circus where he worked or the island of Manhattan which must have offered something more than a circus and a collection of banks.

In some letters he wrote about boats daily vomiting an avalanche of poor people, day after day, onto the narrow streets of New York and none of those poor people spoke English, but Russian or Polish or worse, Italian. "Why worse?" I asked Siora Maria. Because, according to Sior Gino, many did not even speak real Italian as we were taught in Austrian schools, but Sicilian or Calabrese or Neapolitan. What was wrong according to him was that they spoke *only* dialect. We spoke *noneso* at home, but Italian in school.

Actually the immigrants' boats arrived in a little island in the bay of New York which he called Ellis Island and it wasn't clear at all from his letters how these poor people who didn't speak English at all reached the island of Manhattan from the other island. Sior Gino's only worry was that they did not speak English...and left the reader of his letters in the dark on the basics of normal life.

In sum, New York from his letters did not seem to me a city at all, like Trento, but a cluster of scattered islands, one of them at least so overcrowded that people slept piled up one over the other. Worse. People living there didn't know what would happen to them from one day to the next. They all, I thought, must have lived in a terrible state of anxiety about their future, like the wicked people of the world before the Great Flood. Except that God did not preannounce the Flood to anybody except his favorite Noah. From Sior Gino's letters I gathered there was no Noah in New York when he lived there. So the poor immigrants, who didn't speak English at all and who made up the greatest part of New York, lived in constant fear that the worse may still come.

Of course I was not supposed — nor would I have ever dared, for obvious reasons, — to ask Siora Maria any question about or show any interest in New York. Siora Maria was not interested in New York at all. For her, New York represented Gino's by-gone past, never to be visited again, the dark years after the painful separation, the dark, very dark dawn of the century. Now, in 1912, the century was old, at least in America, and life was smiling again upon her beloved in the land of the setting sun.

After a few years in New York, Sior Gino, equipped by now with more than the language of the country, with the desire of breaking through the wall, or 'frontier' as they called it, that separated him from the possibility of making a better living, had moved West across a chain of mountains called "Alleghenies" and had settled in a beautiful city called "Cincinnati" at the confluence of a huge river with two minor ones, near a huge Lake called Erie.

§ § §

Siora Maria and I fell upon Cincinnati because her interest was not in "America" per se but in "Sior Gino's America." And not in his peregrinations before he reached his final goal, but in where he lived *now*, after he had obtained peace of mind and success. Cincinnati as her son's final residence helped Siora Maria to discover America. She lured me along as an enthusiastic companion in her imaginary voyage. After our creation began to take shape, Sior Gino himself joined us first with letters he addressed to his mother, then with most useful information addressed to both of us. Cincinnati became in its last stage a project which all three of us shared across the Atlantic.

§ § §

Cincinnati acquired an identity and existence of its own not long after we had begun our project, with the Ohio River overwhelming the Noce and the Adige or even the Danube in Vienna and the Tiber that flows through Rome.

The speed with which the community of Cincinnati developed its civic, intellectual and artistic life was for us close to a miracle. Thus both Siora Maria and myself, as partners in the discovery in spite of our difference in age, social class, and upbringing, fell in love with Cincinnati's America.

§ § §

Fortunately, the name of the city, Cincinnati, had nothing to do with the aristocratic Roman hero Cincinnatus whom I disliked. Cincinnati got its name from the Society of "Cincinnati" to which the first Governor of the NorthWest Territory, a certain Yves Saint Clair, belonged. It was a society founded by a group of Revolutionary War Veterans originally presided by George Washington himself.

Cincinnati was, when Sior Gino got there, just one year old, an infant city, holding all the promises of a new man! The City had been regularly founded, as Rome was founded by Romulus on the Tiber in 760 B.C., by St Clair on the Ohio River in 1788 A.D. But here the comparison with Rome stopped because Romulus killed his brother so that Rome could have one and only name, whereas Cincinnati at birth had a different name which we liked very much: Losantville. St Clair for some reasons changed the name without any trouble because in America you are free to change your name peacefully whenever you want. Thus wrote Sior Gino.

Even before its regular birth as a city, because of its lucky geographical position, the place had been visited regularly by a French explorer called La Salle, and, after 1750, it had been used as an approach by the Indians. Here we paused again, because Siora Maria knew a lot about the Indians, whom she dearly loved. Since I knew absolutely nothing, I listened in awe to her stories. Her Indians however lived in Mexico at the time of Columbus, long before those of Losantville, and most of them were killed by the Spaniards.

Opposite Losantville/Cincinnati on the Ohio river stood two other towns, Newton and Covington which happened to be in another state called 'Kentucky.' Covington was of particular interest to us because Sior Gino's house rose there, a two story wooden house painted white, on a high stone basement, with a garden in the back. That was around 1905 or later. Sior Gino sent us a picture of it.

After Losantville became Cincinnati in 1790, we saw it prospering overnight as a shipping port for wheat and meat from the prairies. At this point both Siora Maria and I fell in love with steam-navigation. The steam navigation of the Ohio had begun long before Sior Gino's arrival and was vividly described in Sior Gino's letters. He even sent his mother pictures of the steamers. And of himself on one of them.

As early as 1867, a long bridge with towers on both ends — something unheard of for us — was built by a German, much to Siora Maria's dismay, who would have liked to see it the creation of an Italian. Sior Gino, who was in love with that bridge, made it worse for his poor mother when he let her know that much of the civic and cultural achievements of the city were due to German immigrants who accounted for ninety per cent of all foreign born citizens. Most of the people in Cincinnati were foreign born.

"This is an inappropriate conclusion. The Italians must have contributed just as much, but as usual they are not recognized for what they did!" Siora Maria commented. Yet, she agreed with me that if Sior Gino made a successful career in this miraculous community it was because German was one of its two languages, although, it seems, Sior Gino was used by his Bank for his Italian as well as for his German, or perhaps for both. I also reminded Siora Maria that Sior Gino had struck luck in New York when he had stumbled on the opportunity of buying cigars for the German speaking banker. I imagined for a while that Sior Gino's wife Flora, who was Austrian or Swiss, might have eloped West with one of those enterprising Germans over that bridge, perhaps in a covered wagon. I liked the idea. Sior Gino often wrote about covered wagons, never about his wife. Nor did Siora Maria ever mention her.

With equal enthusiasm we both followed the role played by our City in the history of the war against slavery. I was sure slavery was a phenomenon of which we, in our mountains, had lost sight since the advent of Christianity, but Siora Maria insisted that it was practiced all along in Europe until shortly before the American Civil War. In any case, to our great satisfaction Cincinnati played a most decisive role in the antislavery agitation. The City was an important station in the so-called "underground railroad" with many homes opened to escaping slaves. We were delighted to discover that Harriet Beecher Stowe, the author of the novel *Uncle Tom's Cabin*, lived in Cincinnati and had gathered much material for her book there. At this point in our research we dutifully paused to read *Uncle Tom's Cabin*, a copy of which we found in the library of Sior Augusto who, Siora Maria declared with pride, was a friend both of witches and of slaves.

Sior Gino congratulated his mother on her readings. He also informed her that an antislavery Journal "The Philanthropist" was published very early in Cincinnati and its presses were destroyed by the mob, because, as Sior Gino explained, not everybody was a hero fighting against slavery. One of the glories of America was freedom of speech which implied freedom of thought. I preferred to stay clear of this issue, afraid the subject might infringe on the agreement reached between Mare and Siora Maria to keep politics and religion out of our conversations.

Of course Cincinnati sided with the North during the Civil War — a war, we discovered, of unbelievable cruelty, something our part of the world had not experienced since the time of Napoleon. It was even threatened with a Confederate attack and for a while put under martial law, but the Confederates knew better and never came.

By the end of the summer of 1912, Siora Maria and I had reached such familiarity with our beloved City across the Ocean that we could visualize its map, and actually drew one. About half of the City on the plain lies south of the Ohio in the state of Kentucky — we both loved the name! Here were the Covington suburbs with a long river frontage. On the plain streets intersected at right angles. On the hills rose the finest residences, buildings of brick limestone besides those in wood painted white like Sior Gino's house. In the so called 'bottoms' were the factories and the whole-sale districts.

I singlehandedly carried out, on the basis of my personal research and mostly on some enthusiastic information that Sior Gino shared by letter to his mother, a study of Cincinnati's art and music and mainly educational development. Siora Maria was overjoyed by the results of my work which made me feel as if I had something to do with what went on beyond the Ocean.

In relating our valley to Cincinnati, in 1912 both Siora Maria and I realized that our valley had remained, like a rock, more or less the same throughout millennia, with its poor villages and its goats. Changes were hardly brought about by the people themselves, but by an earthquake or a volcanic eruption, a war or a plague. Whereas in Cincinnati it all happened without any earthquake, or any war or plague, and at an incredible speed, all by the imagination, the will and the hard work of *man*. How could that happen? we asked ourselves, but we were too busy discovering to try to find answers.

What surprised me was Cincinnati's ability to solve problems overnight that we hadn't solved yet, like the interrelation of the Catholics with the Protestants, which troubled my old Monsignor. Here was a 'baby-city,' hardly one century old, which — as Sior Gino wrote — housed a Roman Catholic Cathedral near the First Presbyterian Church, which, he said, was just as beautiful. Far from killing each other, the Catholics and the Protestants lived happily together in Cincinnati, as far as Sior Gino knew. I even discovered that in 1831 a certain Bishop founded a St Francis Xavier seminary for training Catholic priests, while nearby a few years before a Lane theological seminary was created to train Presbyterian ministers, which means Protestant priests! Of course I couldn't speak about all this to Mare. It would have probably upset her, or perhaps not at all, because she was for peace and not for murdering Christians. (I knew my Monsignor was aware of and happy about what happened in Cincinnati and happy I did find out about it.)

Banks and Universities in Cincinnati were as important as Churches. The most beautiful buildings housed Banks with strange names like the Fifth Third Central Trust Company, which employed Sior Gino, and the First and Second National Bank, and the Provident Savings Bank and Trust Company. But then, equally important were the Parks, hundreds of them, with lakes and trees and flowers of all kinds, and a zoological garden with all sorts of animals, and Museums and music of all kind, all promoted unfortunately not by the Italians but by the Germans.

§   §   §

In sum, in every field of human enterprise, our Cincinnati was the world's model city. Sior Gino was lucky to enjoy life there, though his wife had given him much trouble from beginning to end. As her last gift, she passed her tuberculosis on to him. But even in this unfortunate case Sior Gino was lucky because in Tajo he would have died, whereas Cincinnati had state-of-the art hospitals where, we felt sure, he would soon be restored to health.

What, however, provoked our unlimited enthusiasm was the fact that in Cincinnati all students were assured an education, *free of charge*, in public schools, from kindergarten to university. And they even had a school for teaching English to immigrants where Sior Gino taught besides working in a Bank.

Cincinnati, Sior Gino wrote, had also started a system of supplementing university instruction by practical training, so that if my family had lived in Cincinnati instead of Tajo my brothers Damiano and Silvio could have attended the university while working at the whip factory and in the fields! And now they could be teachers like me, or priests, or even pharmacists. Even Damiano could have made it to be somebody, dumb as he was. I had the impression that in Cincinnati they took care also of the dumb.

Sior Gino informed us also that shortly before his arrival a university was founded in the midst of wide fields called a 'prairie,' with an observatory to study the stars. It was, he wrote, the first municipal university in America. That university had a medical school and a law school, the oldest one West of the mountains that Sior Gino crossed when he went West. And the university was supported with money from the wealthy — of whom there were plenty in Cincinnati — besides of course with money from taxes.

What did our wealthy families contribute? I asked Siora Maria, without hiding my resentment. She answered without embarrassment that, as the Ohio River could not be compared to the Noce, the wealth existing in Cincinnati had no correspondence in any of the valleys of our region. Our wealthy families contributed to the public good, although not enough. Sior Augusto's family, for instance, supported the classical gymnasium of the Benedictines in Merano. As for her family, the Cianis and the Taxis, the Cianis mostly gave to the national Cause, for the Trentino to be 'redeemed' or 'freed' by Italy. She was aware that that Cause was of no interest to most of us and did not help us in our daily life. Still it was a noble cause. As for the Taxis, she confessed with sadness that her son Tullio, who had married Cornelia Taxis, had engaged in some very bad speculations about hundreds of geese that had then died of starvation. Recently, his wife Cornelia with their four children had returned to live in her parents' home, the home of Baroness Clementina who was also Sior Augusto's sister. That was an embarrassment for Siora Maria and I was sorry to have raised the issue, and assured my friend that, in spite of my admiration for Cincinnati, I would never have given up Tajo and her company, which I immensely treasured.

§ § §

We were still in the process of happily discovering Cincinnati, when on a Sunday afternoon, Siora Maria triumphantly handed to me a letter of Sior Gino. In a few lines written with a shaky hand he said he had decided to complete his convalescence at home near his mother. He would be arriving in Tajo soon.

It was late April 1913. The fruit trees were all in bloom, the air filled with their sweet fragrance, thick carpets of violets pierced the moss around the spring. Siora Maria was in a trance, but I could not share her joy. I feared Sior Gino would deprive me of the company of my greatest friend, of the joys and sorrows we were used to sharing. I was jealous and apprehensive. Sior Gino's contribution to our "Cincinnati" implied his being *there*, but physically unreachable. By being in Cincinnati he gave substance to our vision.

At the same time, I was curious as to what a man who came from Cincinnati looked like in flesh and blood.

# CHAPTER 5

## A White Rose

I usually refrained from visiting Siora Maria when one of her children was with her. From the moment Sior Gino arrived, I put an end to my visits altogether. I had more than enough happening in my own life to keep me busy from dawn until late at night. With my arrival in Tajo I had freed Mare of the heavy responsibilities of the house. My salary had allowed us to complete payment on the mortgage of the house. We could now say with pride that the house was *ours*! For our fortune, my brother Damiano, had married one of the sturdiest women in the village. The combination of the two, my salary and the arrival of Speranza, had assured the family temporary survival.

Speranza, which means Hope, entered our home at the right moment, that is when, with Mare's physical decline, we needed two strong arms to lift heavy weights, an enormous patience besides a will to work from dawn to the *Angelus* and beyond if necessary. She had all these qualities, plus a heart to house us all, her husband included, who unfortunately remained hopeless in spite of his marriage.

Nine months punctually after the marriage, the couple produced a boy whom they called Felice, which means "Happy." The boy turned out to be one of the unhappiest members of the family, a fact which was not evident at birth. Certainly it was not his nor his parents' fault. Felice was undoubtedly born at the wrong time and in the wrong place.

My youngest brother Silvio and I, validly supported by Speranza, launched the household in two enterprises which, had Tajo been on the shores of the Ohio River instead of the Noce, would have freed us forever from the incumbent threat of chronic poverty under which the family had lived as far back as we remembered: our own whip factory and the marketing of the fruit of the valley. The first venture failed, the second bloomed only years after I had left Tajo.

Silvio, who had inherited Mare's physique and her indomitable willpower — he was a tall, blue eyed man with a handsome mustache, adored by all the women in the village —, disdained working in the fields, like Maria, but not for the same reasons.

He made us women accept as a hard fact that the three fields we owned, one at considerable distance from the other, two in hardly reachable locations, produced enough basic food to support us, but nothing more. If one year we had a drought we simply would starve.

"Draw your own conclusions!" he yelled. He never spoke in a normal tone of voice. We were all sitting around the fire in the kitchen on a rainy day in the fall, — Mare, Damiano, Speranza nursing Felice, and myself. Mare reminded Silvio that, besides paying for the mortgage, we had invested some of my money in two robust cows. He sneered. Gone were the happy times of Margherita Bazzochera when a cow made a difference in the economy of the village, he said. In 1913 we needed extra income besides my salary, which, according to Mare, should have been sufficient to 'save us.'

Emma sent us every penny she earned. As for Maria, she had finally crowned her highest ambitions. "I certainly do not intend to die as the house-stewardess of the Albertis!" she had told me once when I had visited her in Trento. And with a big smile, hands on her hips, she had revealed to me that a friend of the Albertis was courting her. He was the pharmacist of Creto, a village of the size of Tajo, but situated in a narrow valley, quite different from the Valle di Non. The Valle delle Giudicarie was down South, at the border with Italy, a kind of narrow crevasse cut among the high mountains which abruptly fall into the widest and most beautiful of all Alpine lakes, the Lake of Garda. At a difference with the Valle di Non and its continuation, the Sun Valley or Valle di Sole, the Valle delle Giudicarie hardly ever saw the sun. That is why during the summer it was the favorite resort of Trento nobility and clergy. Maria's husband was a white haired man twice her age, the pharmacist Giovanni Corazzola. "And so what?" she rebuked me when I asked her if he was healthy. "Healthy or not, I don't care. He can give what I longed for all my life." The pharmacist was, with the parish priest, the prominent character in our villages.

When Sior Gino arrived in Tajo I was about to leave for Creto where Maria had given birth to a baby girl. We all knew Giovanni, as we called him now, was rude and she was obviously unhappy. It was up to me now to discover why.

Before I left home, Silvio announced to us, like Caesar about to cross the Rubicon, that he was starting his own whip factory. For that purpose he was going to carve out a large space in the back of the *Sala*. The *Sala* was the center of our old house, a huge hall, entering the house from the *pont*, on which all rooms opened. Silvio revealed he had taken a loan from a bank for the purpose.

Mare, who rejected the idea of the loan, was silenced by Silvio's shouts. Silvio was the boss from now on, if we liked it or not. I personally agreed with his project. Damiano didn't care. Speranza was silent. She knew her role in the family was *work*, physical, heavy work. Perhaps she hoped the whip factory would lighten her labors. I felt miserable for Mare. From now on my task in the family was to protect Mare from Silvio's blows. He was good at heart and listened to me most of the time, but Mare now stood like a rock between him and his dream.

My stay with Maria in May 1913 was brief and different from my previous visits. In the past, I had been introduced to all the pharmacists in the valley delle Giudicarie by an elderly couple, the Alimonta, steady guests of Maria and her husband, the finest people I had ever met. Their aim was — they used to joke — to find the right husband for me. How did it happen that a handsome and witty woman had no fiancé, when less gifted women my age already had a husband and a child on the breast? Since I was also the best rock climber of the group, they baptized me 'their little goat,' which really pleased me because I still adored goats. What they meant, however, was that I was wild and unapproachable. I answered the Alimonta that my main task at this moment in my life was to get my family out of trouble, and no fiancé could help.

During the present visit there were no Alimonta. It was just the four of us, Maria, the baby, Giovanni and myself in a huge, silent stone house that stood like a rock over a village built on rocks in the dark, narrow valley. Maria's baby girl Rina was adorable, but I immediately sensed something strange going on in this silent empty space. On the first morning after my arrival, Maria showed up at breakfast, her eyes red from crying. Walking the baby in the small garden in the back of the pharmacy, while Giovanni was busy with his customers, she plainly told me that her husband was jealous, not of men around her, but of her very family. He considered us up in Tajo a dead weight on his shoulders. Why?, I asked surprised. Silvio, she said, had asked him for money. He didn't trust Silvio and he was making her pay for it. She opened her beautiful embroidered blouse — a gift of the Albertis, she remarked bitterly — and showed me a black and blue mark near her breast. "He hit me," she said, "while I was breastfeeding Rina."

I got angry at her. Why did she put up with such brutal injustice? I argued, but unfortunately, she was too far gone as the victim of an insensitive husband. There was nothing I could do to help her. I left, heartbroken and helpless.

In Tajo the situation had worsened. Mare received me trembling with rage. One night, upon his arrival back home half-drunk from the pub, she had 'reminded' Silvio in her usual way that he could not pay the mortgage for his whip-factory by spending the nights in the pub. To her horror, he had hurled her into the *Stua* yelling: "Stay quietly where you belong, *maledeta vecla* (damned old woman)." Mare hurled those words again and again in my face as if to call me responsible for the accident. I had difficulty calming her down and was at a loss on how to approach Silvio, when the very evening of my return from Creto something unusual happened.

While I was milking my cows at sunset in the stable under the *pont*, Speranza ran down to me with a cheerful expression on her otherwise impassible face.

"Come," she said, pulling me away from my cow, 'Siora Maria is here. She is sitting with Mare on the *pont*...." Then she added mysteriously: "She brought Sior Gino along!"

I raised my head. There HE was, Sior Gino himself in flesh and blood walking slowly down from the *pont* towards me with a smile:

"You haven't changed a bit," he said in the same mellow Italian as his mother. "You are exactly as I remembered you."

"When and where did you see me?" I asked.

"Where do you think? In my dreams of course!" He laughed. Then completely at ease as if we had just seen each other a few days before, he shook my dirty hand and looking at my apron,

"Soon," he said, "you must show me your cows."

Before I could answer, Siora Maria was with us. She asked me about my visit to Creto. Did I cross the border as I usually did, invited by the Alimonta, to eat dinner in Italy? The food and the wine and the whole atmosphere was so much more enjoyable in Italy than on this side of the border. I told her the truth. She took me by the hand away from the others and in her own very special way convinced me to forgive Giovanni and try to discover how he could improve his relations with Maria. As for Mare and Silvio, there was basically nothing wrong with them. It was a generational conflict. Silvio was a good man who loved Mare. I shouldn't worry. Then she insisted I should visit her as usual. Gino was surprised not to find her with me.

From that day on, our meetings at the Siori's mansion continued as in the past, when my intense work allowed me an hour of relaxation. Yet, I sensed immediately that with Sior Gino's presence life was changing for all of us. He would show up unexpectedly, with a joke, a flower for both of us, a newspaper article, or simply a piece of interesting news. He wasn't physically handsome as some of the boys of the village who courted me. He was an elegantly dressed middle-aged man, verging on the plump. Pale and weakened by his illness, he walked slowly, at times painfully so, as if he didn't have the strength to put one foot in front of the other. Yet, he smiled wistfully and, as time passed and his health improved, he laughed easily.

Shorter in stature and with a beardless round face, Sior Gino lacked his father's solid, imposing presence. Yet there was definitely something of Sior Augusto in him when it came to history, politics, or the natural rights of an individual. He spoke then with ease and pleasure, even passionately. For the time being, his mother and I were his only audience and he kept us spellbound. He wrote as elegantly as he talked, with a thin, regular handwriting, the words slanted slightly to the right.

During our walks together, his well-shaved face, shadowed by an American wide-brimmed panama hat, sparkled with pleasure when conversation fell on subjects that fired his imagination: nature, our lives in the village, the immensity of the ocean he had crossed twice which reminded him of the immensity of the American prairies, friends in the village whom he left as boys and had met now as grown men, friends he had left behind in Cincinnati. One of our favorite topics of conversation was Cincinnati. I never tired of asking him questions about that miracle city which had tied me to Siora Maria in new and unexpected ways. He often said he never felt as close to Cincinnati as when I asked him about it. Although we did not see eye to eye, he never contradicted me, but added details that made that city more real for me. In Cincinnati, Sior Gino had suffered from a severe case of loneliness, in spite of his happy disposition. The village, though poor and primitive, was for him the best possible therapy. I never understood what he meant by that, perhaps because I had never suffered from loneliness, except for very brief instants, like when, at thirteen, Mare abandoned me in Trento. Trento had been hard on me in spite of its beautiful Cathedral. Cincinnati must have been for him like Trento for me. Now we were both happy together in *our* village. This did not mean we were village-bound. Perhaps we needed the village as a basis, a point of reference, in exploring the world. What we had in common was a love for a 'world' that had its roots in our village.

Sior Gino did not physically resemble Siora Maria either, but he definitely shared her joy of living, her curiosity of mind, her repulsion for social conventions, her attraction for all expressions of art, her wit and generosity, and her love for freedom and independence. He also shared her irrepressible interest in every human being regardless of social classes. If we met a farmer during our walks or an old woman, he would not only greet him or her by taking off his hat but would find the proper way to befriend them. When mother and son were together and in a good mood, I did not distinguish one from the other. They both thrived on society.

When the three of us were alone, their witty conversation left me often speechless. Overwhelmed by awe and admiration, I could have listened to them forever in silence, but they artfully led me into their world, making me feel at ease within it. Sior Gino's presence added a new dimension to my life, in harmony with his mother.

Alone with Siora Maria, not long after her son's return, conversation often focused on my suitors in the village and on why I didn't pay attention to any of them. Among them the one who had been for years stubbornly persistent in trying to get my attention and eventually my consent to marry him was the son of the owner of Tajo's only pub and hotel. His name was Beppe Reich. Together with the pharmacist, but definitely several notches lower in prestige, Beppe's father, and now his son as his legitimate heir, enjoyed a considerable reputation in the village. Whereas the pharmacy stood on the main road on the extreme South, the Hotel Reich stood on the far North of the village, close to the mansion of Sior Augusto. A decorous three story building, the most handsome house of the village, the Albergo Reich offered to its guests a dozen comfortable rooms and, in its pub, plenty of wine, mostly the local kind of acidulous red, strong enough to get the young and the not so young of the village drunk on Saturday night. This happened regularly, much to the dismay of the parish priest, Don Beppe, and of Sior Augusto and Siora Erminia when they were alive.

Siora Maria laughed about it, secretly wishing she could enter the forbidden 'place' to paint, whereas Sior Gino had been, during his adventurous youth, a regular customer of the pub and a personal friend of the young Beppe Reich. The gossip was that the young Beppe, as a teenager, had helped Sior Gino, who was older than him, but still young, in his adventurous loves during his months of vacation from the university. *Comare* Maria, the midwife of the village, who was *the* authority on illicit affairs, had told us a story about that on a cold winter evening, while the snow silently enveloped our village. I was then a young girl, sitting in the kitchen near the fire with Mare and Pare.

Sior Gino had spent the last day of his Christmas vacation from the University of Munich having fun with friends, men as well as women in the Valle di Non. He had enjoyed the last night before departure cavorting from village to village on his family sled with four or five friends. He had a pocket full of Kronen, big pieces of gold, enough money to support himself for the next few months in Munich. Sior Gino had spent a few of those Kronen with his friends. He thought he still had most of them in his pocket. When, with the first stars of the new year he stopped the sled outside of Tajo to make sure the gold pieces were still in his possession, he noticed that *all* of the Kronen had vanished, obviously lost in the snow.

Without wasting any time, Sior Gino's good friends from the village began a search of ten kilometers or so of snow-blanketed road between Tajo and Dermulo and Dermulo and Coredo up on the mountain slope. By noon of the New Year young Beppe Reich had delivered all of the lost gold pieces into the hands of a happy Sior Gino. *Comare* Maria loved to embellish this particular story with all the poetic devices she reserved only for the most worthy subjects. She was, after all, the godmother of Beppe Reich besides being a distant family relative and a backstage customer of the pub.

It was common knowledge that from that moment on Beppe Reich became for Sior Gino the heart and soul of the village he loved so much. It was Beppe Reich who welcomed Sior Gino upon his arrival in Tajo from America on behalf of all the villagers. He, not the mayor or the parish priest. The two had been inseparable from that moment on.

§ § §

Perhaps in memory of her son's long friendship with the Reichs, Siora Maria bluntly asked me why I didn't pay any attention to Beppe Reich who distinguished himself for his physical appearance from all other young men. As a painter she loved his tall athletic figure, his handsome face, blue eyes with dark brown hair, besides his happy nature. My reaction was that yes, he was physically attractive, but if my choice of a partner for life had to be made on this basis, I would be forced to consider him only one of the candidates among the several young men available in Tajo, Trento, Segno, Coredo and other villages of our sunny valley, besides Creto in Val delle Giudicarie! We laughed and the subject was dropped with Siora Maria's visible satisfaction. It surfaced again soon after, this time during a meeting with Sior Gino.

§ § §

It was a serene afternoon in the late spring of 1914. I had started my day at dawn joining Speranza in the plowing, since Damiano and Silvio were busy with the whips. I then spent six hours with my children in school. What was on my mind all day was my forthcoming late afternoon visit with Siora Maria.

When I finally rang the bell of the mansion up the hill, she met me downstairs at the door with a big smile and a big book, a Renaissance poem she loved, the *Orlando Innamorato,* in a beautiful illustrated edition. "I would like you to read to me the usual Canto," she said.

Siora Maria loved both poems about Orlando, the one about Orlando in love (*Innamorato*) and the one about Orlando insane (Orlando *Furioso*). The court of Charlemagne, as it had been reinvented in the octaves of two of her favorite poets, Boiardo and Ariosto, had a special attraction for her because of the role love played in the lives not of commoners but of extra-ordinary people, kings and warriors. *Love* and *Magic* were her two favorite ingredients for a novel. She was puzzled by the warrior Orlando — she often said — because this nephew of Charlemagne, the main defender of Christianity against the Muslims, had suddenly changed personality and behavior when he became stricken by love for Angelica, an Oriental Princess who had travelled from the heart of China to Paris, in disguise, in order to lure the best warriors away from Charlemagne, her father's personal enemy. Angelica, besides being a princess, was also a magician and a very astute woman. As astute as Siora Maria when she was Angelica's age, I said at times to myself.

Soon after Siora Maria sat down, brush in hand, to begin work on one of the panels of the door of the *Sala,* Sior Gino entered the room silently. He was dressed in a white summer suit which fitted him perfectly now that he had completely recovered from his illness. He settled on the sofa in the far corner of the room, a journal in hand. Although he whispered to us that he had come to keep us company because he had nothing better to do, it was evident to me that the visit was planned. The thought bothered me, but I decided to pretend it didn't. So, as Siora Maria began moving her brush with wide strokes on the white panel, I began reading aloud from her favorite *Canto*. I had been taught by her not to read but to recite in a high dramatic tone, as if I were on stage in front of a large audience. Although at first, I was embarrassed by Sior Gino's presence, as the story developed it so overwhelmed me that I instinctively identified with each of the two heroes as they dueled in a clearing of a pine forest near a moss-covered spring. That forest for me was "Fontanelle."

Orlando, the greatest warrior of the Christian, that is the civilized world, is happy to duel with Agricane, the King of Circassia, because Agricane is the most valiant warrior of the 'pagan' or Muslim world, the world of primitive forces. As for Agricane, he had gone out of his way to meet Orlando, attracted by his reputation. Although each of the two champions fights nominally for his own 'God' and religion, they really fight for the joy of fighting, knowing that they are the best of all the warriors in the world, and each is full of open admiration for the other. Since, however, they are perfectly equal in strength, the duel goes on for a whole day without any indication of minimal gain of one over the other. So, at sunset, by common agreement, they decide to stop for the night. As they lie side by side on the grass under a huge pine tree, the moon peacefully shining among the stars above them, they engage in pleasant conversation, first over religion, then over education, finally over love. On the religious issue, Orlando tries his best without success to convince Agricane that Christ holds the secret for human fulfillment and success within a world where man dominates nature. Agricane is not interested in God. On the subject of education, Orlando upholds the theory that books improve the quality of a warrior, whereas Agricane proudly boasts of having hurled the books he was supposed to read on the head of his teacher.

When, however, by chance, the two knights discover that they are both in love with the same young lady, the Oriental Princess Angelica, they furiously leap back onto their horses, and engage in a most ferocious duel which ends at dawn with Agricane's death. Both were unaware that the blond Angelica — as astute as she was beautiful – loved neither of the two, but was instead using them both for her own secret purposes. The two come very close to each other in the end when Agricane before dying asks Orlando to baptize him. Orlando crying over the dead hero, out of admiration and respect, leaves his body untouched in full armour, sword in hand.

§ § §

When I raised my head from the book, Siora Maria had stopped painting. Both her and Sior Gino were visibly moved by my reading, much to my embarrassment. Then Sior Gino asked his mother if he could take me to Fontanelle with him.

"It is up to her!" Siora Maria smiled to her son.

As we walked side by side past the flowerbed where the year before we had sown the 'American roses,' Sior Gino held me gently by the arm. Then he recited by heart the two final octaves of the *Canto* I had just read. He spoke not in the dramatic tone I had learned from Siora Maria but in a quiet low voice as if the story of Orlando, Agricane, and Angelica was part of our everyday life, not a drama invented by a poet for our amusement.

I told him so and he replied that, yes, Orlando's story deeply moved us today, four hundred years after it was invented, because it dealt, through poetry, with basic human passions, that is love, hatred, jealousy, mainly love for life. Orlando and Agricane were both in love with life.

Then he jokingly asked me which one of the two was my favorite.

"I love both," I answered. "For me they are one and the same person. Agricane after the duel will live forever within Orlando."

"I was afraid," he replied, "that as a teacher in a devout catholic country such as Austria you would lean for Orlando against such an insubordinate student as Agricane! I am happy you don't."

We had by now reached the wood of "Fontanelle." We sat on the stone bench where Siora Maria and I had spent so many happy hours together, often talking of Sior Gino. He spoke about our meetings with a tinge of envy in his voice, as if he had missed out on something important for his life.

"You know how much my mother means to me," he said, "how I missed her and... how grateful I am to you."

I wanted to stop him but he didn't let me.

"Yes, you do. I am more than grateful for all that.... I wish I could do something for you... for your future...."

"There is nothing you can do that I cannot do for myself...." I said, and I wished I hadn't.

"There is a young man in the village," he continued ignoring my upset, "for whom I have the highest esteem, who assures me he could make you happy for the rest of your life.... That is, he would like to marry you...."

I was caught by surprise, dumbfounded. Why did mother and son agree to mingle in my own private affairs? I could hardly control my anger.

"I know all about it," I said, "and I say *No* to you as I said to your mother.... I know you will not ask me why, but if you really insist I can give you the reasons, one by one, why I don't want to marry him. First, because my family needs my help, then because...."

He cut me short as if he didn't care for the reasons. His mind was elsewhere. His eyes on the spring, he was absorbed by his inner thoughts:

"Listen to the water," he said, "gurgling out of our spring. That water will soon be far away from us, flowing into a torrent, a river and finally the sea...."

"Did your mother tell you...?"

"Now for once" he turned to me smiling, "let us talk to each other without invoking my mother's presence between us.... Is there a man in the world you would marry?"

I uttered unconsciously the first words that came to my mind: "I will marry the man who sings in my heart."

The church bells started to ring the Angelus.

"I'll walk you to church" he said, helping me to get up from the bench. "We'll join your mother there...."

§   §   §

Next day, on my desk in school I found a white rose laying on a white envelope. After the children had gone, I tore the envelope open. Instantly, holding rose and note close to my throbbing heart I ran down the stairs straight to Santa Maria. Gino was standing there under the tallest linden tree. I fell into his arms.

The note said: "May I aspire to be *that* man?"

# CHAPTER 6

## Sarajevo

In May 1914 I finally became aware that throughout my entire life I had been longing for Gino. Now I knew it. I was free to bloom with the flowers and sing with the birds. In my village in May there was plenty of both. From that moment on, Gino and I filled the rare moments we were allowed to meet alone with all the love that we both had for life. Life suddenly had taken for us such wide-reaching proportions that at times we both felt dizzy, as if we had reached the top of the highest mountain in the world. Nothing around us had changed. It was up to us to change the world. We knew we would because our outlook on men, things, events, had widened immensely since we had joined forces. What I had always admired in Gino had become part of myself. And there was nothing in him I did not admire. His brief daily notes — at times several in one day — were dew on thirsty flowers. I needed them to water my soul. I religiously collected his white roses, which I found in the most unexpected places. The echo of his laughter followed me everywhere.

"I want to make you laugh. You are at your best when you laugh," he whispered to me one evening in church. He almost succeeded in making me laugh in church and in the presence of Mare.

Mare was indeed surprised to see Siora Maria's American son show up in church at the *Angelus* that first night in May when he had led me to church from "Fontanelle."

"What's wrong with the man?" she asked herself aloud, while we slowly walked home, Mare leaning on my arm. I kept silent, breathing in every bit of the warm fragrant spring evening. I was at that moment too happy to give her an answer she would not have liked to hear.

Then, after a while, as Gino joined us in church regularly every night, she seemed to take his company as a natural phenomenon. She never suspected that Gino and I were in love to be married. And I was relieved and worried at the same time. Mare's reaction to our plans was the only cloud in my blue sky. I knew only too well the reasons why she would oppose our marriage. My salary was, for the time being the only steady income for the family. Apart from this very real financial consideration, there was an equally serious emotional one. Mare, whose physical and mental strength had rapidly declined, was infinitely proud of my achievement. I was for her much more for than a successful daughter. I had reached the aim she was unable to achieve in spite of her tremendous efforts. Equally important for her was the fact that the reputation of her old family — the one she still considered her 'real' family — which had slowly waned after she married her handsome, honest, hardworking but dull cousin Pero, was rising again because her daughter, with the help of St. Joseph, her namesake, and the support of Siora Erminia, was now finally one of the three teachers of her village. She was proud of me simply for being a Teacher, because of what that meant in her village, not because I was openly recognized as the best of the three.

On my part, I was deeply aware of and grateful for the enormous sacrifice she had personally made 'to give me an education,' as she put it, and I accepted what that meant for her: a means towards a very well-defined end that had to do only partially with myself as an independent individual. It would break my heart to destroy what I sensed was in this moment the basis of her very existence. Gino understood this issue better than anyone in the world. It was by discussing it with him that it became clear in my own mind. Mare perhaps intuited that she had in Gino the best possible ally, but she never let us know.

The real impediment to a possible solution, we both recognized it immediately, was that Gino had arrived from America penniless and was now being supported by Siora Maria. He had a good job in Cincinnati, but that meant for us crossing the Ocean, this time for real, without much hope of ever returning to the village. I was suddenly terrified at the thought and could hardly hide my fears from Gino. Cincinnati was not Trento. How would Mare survive my departure? How would my 'home' survive without my physical presence? How would I survive without my village?

We agreed one evening in a hurry, after one of my sessions with Siora Maria, that, since we could not go on forever in hiding, we should announce our engagement officially at least to Gino's family, which we thought would be, if not favorable, at least neutral to it, asking them to keep it to themselves until I had informed my own family. I had already told Speranza, who was closer to me than my own sisters Emma and Maria, in part because both lived away from home. She was delighted for me but very apprehensive for the consequences my marriage would have for Mare.

Siora Maria was of course more than happy of our engagement, of which, she openly admitted, she had dreamt for a long time and to which she had largely contributed — and she saw no difficulty in arranging a semi-official family dinner with the excuse of her son's birthday. This was precisely the kind of surprise event she loved to organize.

All of her children showed up in Tajo the day before the party with their husbands and children: Gemma with her husband Emanuele, the son of a farmer of the upper valley who had become worthy of marrying a Siora because of his success as an engineer/architect (he had installed the electricity in the valley and built a streetcar to replace the stage-coach); Clodia with her husband, the well-known lawyer, Giuseppe Cappelletti; Tullio and his wife Cornelia Taxis, from whom he had separated because of his recent venture with the starving geese; Antonio now married to a Cornelia, the pharmacist's daughter. They had brought with them all of their children: Tullio and Cornelia Taxis four, Clodia six, Gemma three. Antonio and Cornelia were expecting (in time they would produce four).

To the great surprise of Siora Maria — not of Gino who had lived an analogous confrontation once before — the dinner was the first of a series of humiliations inflicted by his family on him and, mainly on me, as punishment for having accepted Gino's offer to be his wife.

I was received with courtesy. But from the aperitif to the dessert which concluded the dinner "in honor of Gino," I was made aware that, in principle, there was no intention on the part of a few at least of his brothers and sisters to distinguish between me and Gino's previous wife. Gossip had a basis of reality. Gino was a transgressor of the social conventions the Siori Panizza considered an intrinsic part of their noble inheritance. He had made mistakes in his life for which he had dearly paid. In spite of all his transgressions, he frankly deserved better than what he had chosen the second time around.

Was he stupid, naive, or simply a rebel? They suspended judgment on him mainly out of respect for Siora Maria, who, everybody knew, was a rebel by nature. Yet Siora Maria, being a baroness Ciani, could afford acting as she did. Moreover, being a woman, the damage she could cause the family was limited. But Gino, a man who carried full responsibility for the family's name, constituted a potential risk for the future of the name he carried.

Of course nothing was said against either of the two, Gino or me, but there were enough innuendos to make Gino, Siora Maria and me aware of how the "family" judged the prospective marriage: at best, a necessary evil.

Siora Maria disappeared in her apartment before the dinner was over, visibly overwhelmed with pain. In taking me home under a starry sky, while the crickets' happy song rose all around us from the fields, Gino was as distant from what had happened as he was tender and gentle to me. He spoke calmly and firmly:

"There was unfortunately not much new in what happened in my 'home' tonight. I was sadly confirmed in what I knew.... I have known my family for a long time. My mistake was to expose you to the risk of getting acquainted with a fact that I have learned to accept.... They have ceased hurting me a long time ago, but I realized tonight again, as I did once upon a time, how they can hurt.... I forgive them because they do not know the world is changing under their eyes. They live in a world of their imagination that a whiff of strong wind can blow off without their noticing...."

§ § §

"From now on," he hesitated a moment but then moved on with a firm voice, "remember that if something serious were ever to happen to our family, yours and mine, you can only count on *your* family, no matter how poor they may be."

He was his usual happy self by the time we entered our kitchen where everybody had gathered after the *Angelus* for the evening prayers.

"I want you all to rejoice with us," he said, as we entered the kitchen, in his melodious Italian, "because Beppina and I are engaged to be married."

There was a long pause. Everybody's eyes were on Mare. In the general silence little Felice, who was just learning to walk, escaped from his mother's arms and stumbled across the kitchen. Gino picked him up and held him tight: "Hello, big boy!" he greeted him and the boy hugged him. Silvio, who was a bit drunk as usual, got up and moved straight towards Gino:

"A lucky man you are, Sior Gino," he said, grabbing Gino's hand like a comrade in arms. I was embarrassed. Damiano and Speranza had their eyes fixed on Mare.

Mare stood immobile, her face impenetrable, her eyes looking in the distance as if communicating with an invisible somebody, like after Pare's death.

Gino gently led me towards her: "Mother," he said with the same sweet and caressing Italian with which he had recited that memorable evening in May the stanzas of Boiardo's poem, "Mother," he repeated louder to call her attention, "we are both here to ask you for your blessing!"

He leaned down towards her, took her rugged hand in his and brought it to his lips. She turned her eyes to him in surprise, as if she had been until then somewhere else.

"You *have* my blessing, Sior Gino," she said in Italian, a language she almost never spoke, "and with mine the blessing of your zia Erminia who dearly loved you."

Then she held me in her arms and, for the first time in her life, as far as I could remember, she cried.

§ § §

From that evening on, Gino identified with our problems and, with Silvio and me, discussed ways of solving them. Mare appeared calm, but nobody knew for sure. She spent long hours in silence sitting on the *pont* like Pare used to do, rolling the grains of her big olive rosary through her crooked fingers. It was a rosary made out of olive bones from olive trees grown around the church of St Francis of Assisi. That was the rosary she had received from Siora Erminia after her return from Rome, inconsolable after the premature death of the little Stefano, Gino's older brother.

Around the middle of June, Maria wrote from Creto that her child Rina was ill. She asked for my help. I promised her I would join her as soon as classes were over. The truth was, my whole self was now taken by what was happening to me and to Gino. We suspected that some of Gino's relatives in Trento were working backstage to stop Gino from marrying me. Gossip in Trento and in the Valley described me as a greedy person looking for a rich husband, even a kind of witch visited by the devil. I was deeply hurt. Something within me revolted against the absurdity of the humiliation to which I was subjected. Hurt and helpless, and thus an easy prey to attacks from anonymous sources, I, who had always been open to the world around me, suddenly withdrew into my little corner to brood about myself and the unjust treatment to which I was subjected. Siora Maria was the first to become alarmed by my withdrawal- which I did my best to hide from Gino. Saddened, she ran to Mare. They talked for a long time sitting one near the other on the *pont*. Then Siora Maria spoke for both.

Maria's call for help — she remarked in her obstinate desire of finding a drop of good in a heap of evil — came at the best possible time. School was over. Speranza and Damiano would take over the fields. There would be nothing urgent for me to do in Tajo. Leaving my village for a while would help release some of the pressure I had been subjected to during the recent months and gain an objective perspective on recent events. Gino agreed with them and offered to accompany me to Trento from where I would take the stage coach to Valle delle Giudicarie, down south, near the Italian border.

§ § §

## Mamma in her Village 95

Maria turned out to be precisely what I needed. She loved me, took pride in me, and shared my feelings of resentment from her own perspective. Rina's illness called for the sun which hardly penetrated the valley where Creto was buried. Luckily, only one row of mountains separated Creto from the Lake of Garda where the sun shone at its best. Maria took Rina and me to Sirmione, a small old Roman town sung by Catullus and Vergil centuries before Goethe, a charming village nestled on a peninsula of the southern side of the Lake. (I had learned all about it from Siora Maria).

Sirmione was in itself a divine gift for me in my present circumstances, with its palm and olive trees, its clusters of old Italian-style houses huddled together between the high mountains and the wide Lake that changed colors according to the time of the day. Sirmione and Maria.

Maria, helped free me of the negative feelings that had so far oppressed me by sharing them from her down-to earth positive perspective. Having spent years in the house of the Albertis, she was well aware through gossip of Gino's youthful love adventures. Like the maid who had revealed Gino's story to me, she had approved at one time in the past— in the abstract — of Sior Augusto's harsh decision. Now that Gino had become for her a real human being, soon to be her brother-in-law, her personal perspective towards him had changed radically. Why should Gino's sisters and brothers follow in the old pattern that Sior Augusto himself must have regretted before his death? Times *had* changed, as Gino had told me. That poor wife of his would be judged differently today, even in Trento. Besides, what did I have in common with her? I, the pearl of our household! Maria was mainly angry at the humiliation I had personally suffered at 'that' dinner in 'that' mansion. She embraced me, tears of anger in her eyes and decided I should forgive but definitely not forget. Gino, as I described him to her, deserved to be forgiven. To forget would be a blow to my dignity.

The means to free myself was self-evident: I had to let myself go: to live life in Sirmione as best I could. This was the first moment of relaxation and pure pleasure I had experienced so far in my life, something I had never hoped for, not even in my dreams. Beyond words grateful for it, I treasured every instant as if it were my last breath: a walk under the sun along the "Lungolago," a sunset, the changing colors of the lake, a happy laughter at dinner, the taste of a glass of dark Barolo, as dark as the eyes of little Rina and, most delicious of all, the memory of my short but intense experiences with Gino, which had made me aware of how beautiful life can be. Those memories by themselves made the sun shine brighter.

Maria and I held our most intimate conversations on a beach, while helping Rina build sand castles. At our back, mountains as high as one could imagine plunged abruptly into the turquoise water. Our old village was a prisoner beyond those mountains. South of the Lake, the vast Italian fertile plain meant freedom for us, an opening towards the sea.

To make the best of our stay, our friends, the pharmacists Alimonta, joined us soon after our arrival with some of their friends. We spent every evening together eating often at the 'Caffaro,' a restaurant at the border between Italy and Austria. We also climbed the Val di Bagolin in search of a special restaurant Sior Ernesto Alimonta loved. Dinners there dragged on long into the night because the pharmacists had such a store-room of jokes to tell, we never had time enough to laugh.

§ § §

It was during one of these delightful evenings, sometime in July, 1914 that Gino suddenly appeared among us. He told us, much to our surprise, that he had never gone back to Tajo after he left me in Trento, but, having discovered that I was in Sirmione, he had decided to take up residence at the home of friends in Malcesine on the Lake of Garda, not far from Sirmione. He wanted to "breathe my very same air," he said, without making his presence physically felt by me. I was to perceive his presence in the blue air of the Lake. He smiled at me with such tenderness I felt like embracing him.

"I thought you needed a period of time away from your village and I knew Maria with little Rina and the Alimonta, in the paradise of Sirmione, were too great a miracle to hope for, the ideal combination of beauty and love that you needed to regain your happy active self before we start together our long walk through life. I looked at you all from nearby, from a cove of our lake, with a little envy and suddenly with great apprehension."

§ § §

He stopped abruptly, his face suddenly expressionless as I had never seen it before. His voice reached us from a different world. I was terrified, my heart frozen, my hands trembling.

He had hoped until recently — he said – that we could be married before the end of 1914. He had hoped until recently, he repeated, but now we were suddenly deprived of all power of decision.

There was silence. The blood throbbed violently in the veins of my throat. I could hardly breathe.

§ § §

"Now *Sarajevo* stands between us and our plans."

I was relieved. Sarajevo was totally unknown to me. How could this unknown entity, a somebody completely unrelated to us stop us from fulfilling our desires?

"Who is this *Sarajevo*?" Maria asked, visibly annoyed at the fact that somebody could spoil our moment of joy. Ernesto Alimonta whispered to us that it was not a man but a city in Bosnia. Anyway, how could a so-far-unknown city in Bosnia, destroy our happiness? Maria insisted.

On June 28 — Gino reminded us — the Crown Prince of Austria and his wife on an official visit to Sarajevo had been shot dead by a Serbian anarchist called Princip.

And so what? Maria intervened. There was some talk among men. Ernesto Alimonta described the Serbs as the violent counterpart of their cousins, the Russians. Yet the Serbs were soon abandoned, and talk turned to the consequence of the criminal act one of them had committed. Gino wasn't interested in the Serbs. What worried him were the consequences of the insane act committed in Sarajevo, mainly the confusion in Vienna where Emperor Franz Joseph was readying himself for a war against Serbia, although hardly anybody, he said, was willing to follow him. Italy would most probably keep neutral inspite of the Alliance with Austria, Gino said with evident satisfaction. He was, we all knew, pro Italian like the Alimonta's, but an American citizen. Maria, the Alimontas and I were Austrian citizens and our fate was to be decided shortly by the emperors of Russia and Prussia, and consequently by the governments of England and France.

At this point, Gino also said that he wished he had left with me for America back in June — although he doubted America could keep out of the conflict if the whole of Europe was being dragged into it. America, he told us, had fought at the onset of the century what at the start looked like a noble war to free Cuba and the Philippines from Spanish colonial oppression and turned out in the end to be a bloody Spanish American war not justifiable by the principles of the American constitution. That war — he said — was in the end a warning for a democracy that treasures its Constitution. Even the Women Temperance Union (that is the women against wine) had marched on the streets to protest the atrocities of the U.S. Army in the Philippines.

"A war, no matter how justifiable it looks at the start," Gino concluded with anger in his voice, "gets easily out of control. Leaders of democratic countries in the twentieth century should at all cost avoid entering a war. That's what our so-called Emperor unfortunately did not seem to understand…."

"Who needs an Emperor today anyway?" he burst out in anger, "when the inventions of free men have given the people of the world electricity, cars, trains, planes, and opened entire new continents? When countries like America can be governed by the will of their people?… An Emperor is an anachronism…. But there he is in Vienna our so-called Emperor, a little man incapable of controlling his own personal feelings, playing Russian roulette with millions of people of his so-called empire that covers half of Europe…."

There was silence after his outburst, a silence of approval not of fear.

Given the recent technological developments — Gino continued with the Alimonta's enthusiastic support — nobody knew what kind of war this could be, how it would be fought with so many new arms available, including gas and chemical weapons. How many people would be killed, miserably murdered.... Yet, unless Prussia and Italy agreed to join Austria, Austria per se could only fight a very circumscribed war, that is punish Serbia but nothing more. The war in this case would be an internal fight within the Austro-Hungarian Empire. However, that looked like too simple a solution, given the personalities in question — Franz Joseph and some of his advisors. Besides, Russia would never abandon to their destiny its Serbian cousins. Whatever the scenario, we were left at the mercy of Franz Joseph, whom Gino definitely did not trust....

"The only satisfaction, we, intelligent members of his constituency, can claim is that our Emperor and the Czar and the Kaiser will dig their own grave if they start a war... a meager satisfaction for those of us who will survive," Gino concluded sadly.

§ § §

Though overwhelmed by an anguishing feeling of helplessness, I experienced a new outburst of love for the aspect of his personality I had discovered, thanks to Sarajevo. As he spoke I had detected in him a new natural gift, a new source of energy, a precious quality that no man I had met so far seemed to possess. He could look way beyond our own personal problems, into the problems of the world. Way beyond our village, his family and even my family, even beyond me. And he certainly was a great orator, even better than Sior Augusto! I wished he had enjoyed now, here, his father's power and authority.

At that moment I had an intuition, a passing flash, of what had caused Gino's past troubles in Europe. He had enjoyed life but never fought for success, and therefore had never had access to any form of power. When hit, however, he had reacted with strength and dignity. He had given up Europe and faced the unknown. My admiration for that act of dignity cancelled all recent resentments for his family's behavior towards me. What right did I have to feel resentful when he had overcome all forms of resentment? I was now free to love him and joyfully ready to fight at his side for the success he deserved, now, here, in Europe, in our own village, in Trento and beyond. As I became aware of this new dimension of our relationship, I felt within me a surge of the energy needed to move fearlessly beyond barriers into the world. Had he asked me that night to cross the Ocean with him I would have joyfully consented. But he didn't.

That very night after dinner as Gino and I walked arm in arm along the beautiful *Lungolago*, under a luminous full moon, I tried to explain to him what I had experienced as I listened to him talk, and I naively asked him to help me move along the new road opening in front of us. He laughed and squeezed my arm.

"Who would ever presume to teach you anything, my dear," he whispered tenderly, "is out of his mind. I marry you because I want to learn from you."

§ § §

I had heard of war only through history books. Mare and Pare and their parents had never had the experience, and, therefore, did not speak about it if not in general terms, like the plague.

War was for me now a huge cloud that suddenly darkened the blue skies of Sirmione, that is our own personal life as we wanted to live it, a mysterious phenomenon like an earthquake or the eruption of a volcano, against which there was no defense. We stood for weeks helpless, blindly hoping a miraculous wind would blow the dark cloud away. But it didn't. Without our being aware of it, the big *War* was over us, like a hurricane, yet different from it. It came suddenly and then lingered for four long years, eating away at our flesh like a cancer, until it succeeded in uprooting our very own world and radically changing our lives.

§ § §

Between August 4 and 14, or perhaps before, I do not remember exactly, our Emperor took the great decision. Maria, Rina and I hurried back to Creto on a special carriage rented by the Alimontas.

All means of transportation had been requisitioned for military purposes. Gino had left on his own with the car of a friend, promising me he would try to reach Tajo as fast as possible and somehow help my brother Damiano, who fell within the age of the draft, before he disappeared into the void, swallowed by the Austrian army that was rapidly moving to fight 'our' enemies on different fronts. We didn't know as yet who our enemies were.

By the time we reached Creto, the mobilization of the whole army had been declared and was being reinforced. All the church bells in the narrow valley rang every hour on the hour, their long echoes a lugubrious omen; novenas were held in churches at every hour of the day, attended mostly by elderly women. All carriages were requisitioned for the transportation of the recruits — men between 18 and 42 — as were the few cars that could be found. My separation from Maria and Rina was extremely painful. We were torn apart by forces beyond our control. Would we ever see each other again? My thoughts were with Damiano, horrified at the idea I would not see him again.

I had obtained, by bribing the conductor, a place in a stagecoach overcrowded with recruits, directed to Trento. As soon as they were collected, rapidly put in uniform and armed, they were shipped away by train nobody knew where, but there seemed to be general agreement that they were sent in part to the border of Galicia, in part towards Serbia. There was general confusion among the recruits, but the mood prevailed that within two months at most the war would be won. I looked at those young men as innocent and ignorant victims of forces beyond them up in Vienna. Gino's words had enlightened me: war is like fire, an uncontrollable force. Once a wood catches fire you can fear for your own house no matter how far it stands from the woods.

A young man with shining black eyes who sat near me, engaging in conversation on what was happening around us, tried to convince me that the situation in Vienna wasn't as simple as I thought, actually as Gino thought, because I was repeating to him Gino's words. He was a student of history at the university of Innsbruck, once attended by Gino.

I seemed to ignore — he said — that Austria had been constantly threatened by the situation in the Balkan peninsula since a Congress in Berlin in 1878, when it was actually threatened by war from Serbia and Montenegro and worse of all, by Russia. Austria feared a unification of the so called Southern Slavs. That's why in 1908 it had incorporated into the Empire the two regions of Bosnia and Herzegovina. Didn't I see that, in consequence of the Italo-Turkish war in 1911-12, unification had almost taken place? That would be the end of all of us.... As he spoke his black eyes shone like carbuncles. Wasn't I aware that Austrian diplomacy had succeeded so far miraculously to avoid a war?

I listened attentively but was not convinced by the student's argument, even if what he said was 'historically' true. Gino's words had stuck to my soul. A war is an uncontrollable force, like fire. I fought back stubbornly and the young man stopped talking. Sadly, he looked out of the coach and soon fell asleep.

The coach kept on stopping abruptly because new recruits stood in the middle of the road asking to be picked up. The coachman had a hard time convincing them that we were overloaded. What was the hurry to rush to a battle-field? The horses could not take it.

Young and not so young men, a bundle of clothes and victuals hanging from a stick on their shoulders, were surrounded by women and children hanging on to them. The children were screaming, the women crying, and some of the men seemed to long to get away from it all, but most were stunned, overwhelmed by the shock of having to leave for the first time the only place on earth they knew. I myself was dejected and if it hadn't been for the thought of Damiano back home, I would have given up my place and stopped to console those women and children.

I can still see in front of my eyes a woman with two babies, one in each arm, surrounded by a cluster of children of all ages, like a bunch of grapes. She stood immobile on the threshold of her house, as we were crossing a village, while a man slowly moved away from them, a rucksack on his shoulders. The man had almost reached the coach, when he changed his mind and ran back to his family, and they all fell on him, and he was buried under them. The coach left without him.

"That is what war is about!" I turned to tell the student who sat near me, but he had pulled a book from his sack and never raised his eyes from it until we reached Trento.

§ § §

Gino was waiting at the stop of the streetcar in Tajo. He didn't even allow me to go home. Damiano had been drafted and taken to Bolzano, Bozen in German, the main city of the German speaking Tyrol, on the Adige valley, 30 km north of Trento. We rushed down our valley by tramway, then up the Adige valley to Bolzano by train, and after much searching discovered Damiano in the courtyard of a huge barrack. He stood in the midst of a group of recruits, who all looked awkward and dumbfounded in their new wool uniforms. A mess-tin in his hands, Damiano waited to be fed, a poor animal ready for the slaughter.

"We must get your brother out of there fast! We must deprive this idiotic war of at least one soldier," Gino whispered to me angrily, as our faces pressed against the iron gates of the barracks.

"But how, how?" I moaned helpless, crushed by the avalanche we called war. I started to cry.

"Certainly not by looking at a courtyard full of helpless soldiers from a closed gate and crying...." He was sure of himself, his mind and body working in unison toward a solution.

"I'll do my best to try to get him out but you must help me. Our job will not be easy," he added, and holding me firmly by the arm, he led me away from the barracks, along roads of a city teeming with noisy young officers in elegant uniforms.

As we walked he explained to me that Austria was fighting this war on a very extended front. The widest and most dangerous front at the moment would be North East of us, in Galicia, against the Russian Army. *Bozen* ("Don't call it Bolzano, for God's sake!" he warned me) had been chosen as one of the headquarters to gather the Süd-Tirolians as soldiers for the Russian front, not because of fear of Italy. For the time being Italy was an Ally of Austria. Personally, though he didn't seem to have much trust in Italy's military power.

Gino hoped Italy would break the Triple Alliance, as it was called, so as to eventually 'free' the Italian speaking Süd-Tirol. I was aware of a strong resistance movement of some "Trentini," that is of enlightened citizens of Trento and of the near-by valleys, to join Italy whose language and traditions they shared. I was also aware that many of those patriots were socialists. Farmers in general did not look at them with a favorable eye.

Up in Bozen, pressed by the reality of saving my brother's life, Gino did not waste precious time in political discussions I had so far cautiously avoided with Siora Maria. He focused exclusively on finding a way to get Damiano out of those barracks before he was packed on a train for the Russian front. As we walked away from the barracks, he pointed at the officers we saw around us. They didn't come from the near-by valleys, he told me. Those officers were good middleclass Austrian gentlemen from Lienz and Graz who had managed to be sent South to collect the poor South-Tirolians for the first fighting units in the Austrian Army. For those officers Bozen was a pleasant destination. Every cultured Austrian longed for the sun of the *GardaSee*, a few kilometers away, and of course of the Italian peninsula bathed in the blue sea....

"*Sehnsucht nach Süden*...You remember Goethe's Mignon," Gino quoted sarcastically,

" '*Kennst das Land wo die Zitronen bluehen*...?' Somehow, unconsciously, those elegant officers might even welcome a war as a diversion to their often uneventful or plain boring lives."

Austria, he said, was a boring, land-locked country, center of a vast empire of many lively people whom the common Austrian hardly knew. Nobody understood how Franz Joseph held those people together. Yet they had stuck together so far.

As we walked on arm in arm, he mused ironically on his own past, speaking more to himself than to me: he had spent years among those young Austrians, as one of them, a university student in Lienz, Munich, Graz, and Vienna. He had waltzed, he remembered, for entire nights with his friends in June 1906 when he finally made it to his law degree at the University of Vienna! Like many of those young Austrians, he had hardly studied, but had had a fine time singing and dancing and chatting away about everything and nothing in the

Bierkellers of Innsbruck or Lienz.... Vienna was different. There was much going on in Vienna when he was there. A world of ideas he wished he could have had a chance to enter. Yet, the Austria he had known was a country without moral stamina, without vision, weakened by conventions. Even religion was a conventional commodity. He also had had a taste of life in the army, a lieutenant in the Austrian Army... Love and America saved him.

"To think that, had I not fallen desperately in love and consequently forced to leave Europe for America," he concluded, amused by his own story, "today I would perhaps act like one of these gentlemen.... Walk around Bozen, showing off my uniform, cigar in mouth, in love with the novelty of a war that saved me from boredom.... But I saved myself in time...." He stopped short and added with some bitterness:

"This war, however, will change all of us while it destroys everything around us."

I realized as he spoke that he, my beloved Gino, was the first person the month-old war had changed, at least in his relationship with me. He had never acted or spoken with me as he did now. Bitterness and irony filled everything he said up there in Bozen. Away from the environment we shared, our village, I was at times in awe, at times afraid of him and puzzled. Was he aware that the war was unearthing his old wounds?

I absorbed every word of his, thirsting for more. Why was he forced to leave for America? What did he mean by "falling in love?" With whom had he fallen in love? What forced him to cross the Ocean? I would have never dared to ask him any question because up there in Bozen I discovered I was more in love with him than ever before. So much in love that poor Damiano risked moving into the background while Gino came boldly forward as he prepared himself to fight for Damiano's freedom in his own way, with his own highly unconventional arms. A soldier who despised uniforms.

Revelations ended abruptly when we arrived — as Gino had planned — at destination: Bozen's Walterplatze, the main square of the City near the main church.

Bolzano/Bozen can be stiflingly hot during the summer, located as it is in a hollow between high mountains, the mouths of the valleys so narrow they hardly allow a breeze to come through. In that particular torrid, oppressive evening in August 1914 even the linden trees in the Waltherplatz stood in dead immobility, exhausted from the heat.

The square, locked in between gothic and rococo buildings and its splendid gothic cathedral with the gothic bell tower, was teeming with Austrian gentlemen in Sunday uniforms, long swords swinging from their side, some milling around, some clustering in small groups and chatting, long cigars hanging from under their imperial moustache. A perfect scene for the brushes of Siora Maria, I marveled looking at them.

"Let us sit down. You seem exhausted."

Before I realized what was happening, he got ahold of two free chairs under the trees of the main Bierkeller at a table occupied by three officers. The officers engaged in a lively conversation hardly noticed our presence at first. "Der Krieg... der Krieg..." That's all I could make out. They laughed loudly and were disturbingly noisy.

"Where do they get their energy with this heat?" I addressed Gino in Italian. He silenced me with a glance.

"No Italian, please!" he whispered in a low voice squeezing my hand. A waiter was approaching.

"Zwei Forst und die englische Zeitung," Gino ordered with an unusual — for me — tone of voice. On a tray with two tall pints of foaming Forst beer the waiter brought both papers, the English as well as the local German one. Gino handed the Bozen Gazzette to me and dove into the English paper, feigning to be oblivious of the world around him. I knew nothing escaped him.

It wasn't long before one of the Austrians turned to Gino in English. As the four men engaged in a lively conversation, we all ingested in joyful conviviality as much Forst as we could stand and I was soon dizzy. I wasn't however so drunk as not to notice that they were frequently toasting Cincinnati, and that their loud English had called the attention of two tall men in a blue uniform and particularly long mustache who must have been two policemen. They watched us for a while from a distance. Then they marched without hesitation to our table. The three officers were asked to leave. Gino was led away handcuffed.

"Wait for me here," he told me before disappearing. There was no emotion in his voice.

§ § §

I waited at the Bierkeller until late into the night. A band played Viennese waltzes, Polish polkas and mazurkas, and Hungarian Czardas. There was much singing and dancing and I was repeatedly asked to join the party with other women. I refused. An officer made an attempt to make me speak, but I was in no mood to engage in any conversation. My German was shaky, my English non-existent. I would have liked to leave but didn't know where to go. I thought of Mare and shivered. What would she think of me sitting in a Bierkeller late at night surrounded by soldiers? I dismissed her from my mind. The image of my brother Damiano, mess-tin in hand, violently filled my entire soul. I knew now where to go. I asked the waiter for directions and headed to the barracks.

I reached the barracks after much meandering through dark streets and even darker narrow silent alleys. At the iron gate, which was slightly open, a man in uniform and a civilian were arguing in a lively tone. The civilian was Gino.

He signaled me not to get close. After some heated talk, the Austrian left and shortly after reappeared accompanied by Damiano. The two joined me only after the guard had vanished. I was hiding behind a corner.

Gino knew of a small Gasthaus not far from the barracks. We spent most of the night there talking to each other in a small room filled with smoke. Gino was smoking incessantly while he was trying to find a legal way to have Damiano employed within Tirol. Damiano wasn't collaborating, he complained, as he filled page after page in his thin elegant handwriting with details he could use to argue the case at the Kommendatur. Unfortunately for our case, what we needed, he said, was the proper kind of connections within the military. He had had exceptional luck with the three officers he had met by chance at our table, all three well-acquainted with Cincinnati, one of them the aide-de camp of a General. They had helped him to obtain a temporary leave for Damiano. By noon, however, Damiano had to report back to the barracks.

Gino worked intensely for the following two days. I hardly saw him. I spent my time at the gate trying to catch a glimpse of my brother. Nothing discouraged Gino but, in the end, he had to give up. He lacked the proper connections. Neither he nor his family had any meaningful contact in the Austrian headquarters in Bozen.

After two days, as we stood outside the barracks where he had been housed, Damiano, along with thousands of farmers from the Tyrolian valleys, was put on a long train directed to Poland. Pushing through the thick crowd at the station we succeeded in reaching him. I grabbed him and held him tight in my arms. Gino had to pull me away. I couldn't give him up.

"Take care of my baby," were his last words as he brushed the sweat from his forehead and the tears from his eyes with the rough cloth of his sleeve. That uniform was way too tight for him, like the suit he wore when Mare took him with me to see Monsignor in Trento.

"I promise I'll personally care for your baby, as long as I live." Gino's voice reached him as the train made its way slowly out of the crowded station. Before a thick cloud of black smoke swallowed him, my dear brother, the faithful companion of my golden childhood, leaned way out of the window and smiled to me waving his big hand as if to say "catch me if you can."

Damiano liked to tease me when he was a boy. He had teased me that way, his big hand out of the window of a puffing train, when he left with Mare from Trento, leaving me behind alone…. That was before Monsignor introduced me into his marvelous world…. Why was Damiano abandoning me then in a strange city, away from my village? Why was that huge puffing monster carrying him back to our village, and why was I being left behind alone, in Trento? Alone in a strange city without him and Mare….

In despair, I ran after the train, pushing people out of the way, screaming "Take me with you." A military policeman tried to stop me but I pushed him aside with the violence of despair. I desperately wanted to go back home, back home with Mare and Damiano. Nobody could stop me anymore.

I did not recognize Gino who was running towards me, his arms wide open. He tenderly held me in his arms, like a mother holds her child, dried my tears with a soft cloth, whispered to me words I did not understand. Soothed by his warmth, I finally burst out crying and sobbed loudly until I relieved my aching heart of the overbearing anguish of separation. Nobody paid any attention to us: as the train disappeared, all that was left on the platform of the station were women as desperate as I was.

§ § §

On the train back home, I asked Gino why they had arrested him and how he was released.

"I didn't mind being arrested. It was useful for our case," he answered dryly. "When we arrived in Bozen I didn't know anybody. I had to break the ice somehow. Create a connection. I learned at the police headquarters where Damiano's unit would be sent and when they would leave. They thought first I was a spy and planned to ship me to Innsbruck. They released me after I produced my American passport. My credibility was validated by one of our three officers who showed up where I was held, shortly after my arrest. It was because of that officer that I obtained Damiano's release for one night. He obtained it from his General.... His father still lives in Cincinnati."

# CHAPTER 7

## The War Kills My Village

A few weeks after his departure from Bozen, we were informed by the Kommendatur that Damiano had been killed with most of his comrades in the first great battle on the Russian front.

"Murdered," Gino muttered as he read the news sent to Mare and explained to me that the battles of Uhnow, Rawa-Ruska, Grodeck, followed by the precipitous withdrawal of the Austrian Army in September down to the Carpatian mountains had most of our young men killed or taken prisoners, because they were fighting with inferior arms against the superior Russian artillery. Almost all of our young Tyrolian men were uselessly sacrificed, killed, lost or drowned in the rivers of Galicia.

The news of Damiano's tragic disappearance was still deeply felt in the family when 18 year-old Silvio was drafted and placed among the "Stammschutzer", a division of the Army trained to break frontlines. During the spring of 1915, relations with Italy had worsened. When Italy declared war to Austria, our valley found itself at the front-line. Silvio's division was moved to the nearby Tonale pass to feverishly dig trenches among the glaciers.

There were now three women left to keep the family going: Emma, whom we had called home from Trento, Speranza, and myself. Mare stood silently among us, a giant made helpless by the war that had deprived her of one son after the other, filled her home with overbearing soldiers and starved her and her family. She had never adjusted to the sad fact that she had lost control of the situation. She was too old and too tired to stand the blow.

Emma, Speranza and I were overwhelmed by her sudden silence. Mare's voice had been, throughout our lives, a common point of reference within the village where we were born and grew up. And now she was dead while still alive, a gigantic body without that inner strength that had made of her a leader in her village. She was slowly dying along with her village.

§ § §

It was at this tragic moment that Gino entered the family, as his aunt, Siora Erminia, had done more than once when I was a child. He helped us, as Siora Erminia had done, while holding Mare's hand, that is giving her the feeling, as much as possible, that she was still in charge. All of us, the surviving women, were grateful that Gino had taken Mare's place without her noticing. He was the new point of reference for the whole family.

After having lost Damiano, we were about to lose Silvio. The Tonale Pass, where Silvio was held as a *Sturmschutzer*, was high among the glaciers at the end of the Val di Sole, which is the continuation of the Valle di Non bordering with Italy, our new enemy. The Tonale Pass was a dangerous spot on the southern front. Soldiers died up there daily by the hundreds of wounds and of the equally painful "white death."

"We will get him down from up there," Gino promised, sitting among us around the fire in the kitchen. And he laughed as usual, a sure signal for me that he meant every word he said.

"We'll deprive our Imperial Army of one more soldier to fight against Italy. And this time we will succeed."

We all admired Gino's moral strength, his quiet persistence and his evenness of temper. He never raised his voice nor lost his sense of humor. He even knew how to control his deep-seated hatred for what he called 'this Austrian war,' which allowed him in unexpected ways to gnaw away at the great giant. No matter what happened around us, Gino never lost his optimism, his faith in us or in himself. He was never afraid of death or suffering for himself. At the same time he never missed an occasion to make fun of heroes. "In this war," he would often say, "I want to be the last one to die or not die at all. I am fighting to survive this war and enjoy life with my wife forever in peace."

"How can you be so calm when our own world, what we love and believe in, is crumbling all around us?" I would ask him at times.

"Think of our future family, our life together, our children, thriving in a world forever without wars," he would answer with a bright smile in great seriousness.

Gino was unconquerably stubborn in his faith in a world without wars. Did he truly believe in it or did he pretend to in order to help us, I asked myself as I started off from Tajo on a dreary day, across the woods teeming with soldiers, up our valley towards Fondo and the main town, Cles. I walked slowly and cautiously, loaded with kilos of butter to be delivered on Gino's behalf to a friend of his who was the District Captain in Cles.

As I walked hour after hour, each of Gino's words played like music to my ears. Gino did not believe, like most of us, in the incorruptibility of the Austrian administration. For him, everybody who didn't live by an ideal, was corruptible. In his astute plans, this 'incorruptible' Austrian administrator, the District Captain in Cles, would accept the butter and get soldier Silvio down from the altitudes where he was too close to the gods.

Gino was right. Silvio did indeed descend from the glaciers and serve, as long as the butter lasted, as a chef down south in a military hospital in Valle delle Giudicarie. And when, because of a butter shortage, he was shipped back to the icy Tonale, Gino's awareness of human weakness — this time involving the penchant of a doctor, friend of the family, for a pretty young girl in the neighborhood — succeeded in making soldier Silvio glide down once again from the Tonale Pass through the whole valley, miraculously landing in his own village. His presence, according to a new law Gino had discovered, was declared indispensable for the survival of the agricultural enterprise he had started before being drafted.

We women stood in awe at what Gino could do and were of course overwhelmed with joy at Silvio's presence back home. Mare refused for a while to recognize him as Silvio. She called him Damiano.

§ § §

One day, however, the war caught up with Gino, who was beyond the age of the draft, besides being an American citizen. That was a sad day not only for me, but for the whole family and all the villagers whom he cared for in a personal, individual way. Every individual for Gino was worth an army. Silvio was by no means the only young man of Tajo 'saved' by him.

§ § §

In August of 1915 Gino often sat in the morning on a bench in a corner of the shadowed little square of Santa Maria which was busy as usual with soldiers. Dressed in a white shirt and trousers, he held court with the soldiers, those very same soldiers whom the whole village hated.

Gino attracted the soldiers who had invaded our village like flowers the bees. He was the only person around with whom those poor souls could communicate, he said. Most of them spoke every language on earth, except those that the villagers thought a human being should speak — Italian and German. Only Gino, among us in the village, had developed during this war the miraculous capacity of distinguishing the strange dialects those soldiers spoke. Only Gino could identify an individual language and, by making wise use of Sior Augusto's library, with the help of grammars and dictionaries, could then engage in an elementary conversation with soldiers whom he discovered were Poles, Czechs, Hungarians and different kinds of "Southern Slavs."

According to Gino, the "Southern Slavs" were the most dangerous to the Empire. The young anarchist Princip who had killed our Crown Prince was a "Southern Slav." No matter how good our Emperor was and how perfect his administration, each of these people, he told us, longed for its independence from Vienna — the Southern Slavs most of all.

By allowing those soldiers to express themselves and at times even by writing for them a simple letter home, he was doing a service to a 'human cause.' It was, on his part, a recognition that "human beings" existed even outside the perimeters of our village, he patiently explained to those of us who wanted to listen. A recognition that even if the soldiers now in Tajo were different from us, it did not imply that they didn't have a home, somewhere in the wide Empire, a mother, a wife, children…like us.

He usually closed his informal talk to the small crowd of villagers gathered around him by reminding them that most of these soldiers were spending with us the last days of their lives. The poor men were heading from our village directly to the front lines, where they had a minimal chance of survival. It was a crime on our part to be cruel to them. Since most of the villagers who had not been drafted stayed as far as they could from the front, they had difficulty in understanding what Gino meant when he spoke like that. Yet such was the power of his eloquence and the influence he exercised with his convictions that they listened to him. We all marveled at how the soldiers who were so overbearing with us acted with him. They loved him!

Siora Maria's admiration for everything her son did or said was boundless. Her enthusiasm and desire to help him prompted her by instinct to openly stand by him. Forced by circumstances against her will to strictly keep backstage and inactive at the very moment when 'something could be done,' she had lost her natural liveliness. When I visited her up in her mansion, to which by now she was confined, I was heartbroken to find her totally spent, a butterfly with damaged wings, a bird who couldn't fly, a flower dying of thirst. To make things worse — she revealed to me with tears in her eyes — her daughters were watching over her, organizing for her frequent excursions to Tajo from Trento where they lived, in fear, they said of their mother's very life. Why did they refuse to understand that by so doing they killed life within her? Although Siora Maria made fun with me of their unwanted protection, which she called '*sorveglianza paramilitare*' (paramilitary surveillance), she admitted to herself that in Tajo the risks of her 'falling into traps' and being arrested was real. Gino was the first to make sure his mother kept at a distance from him.

Now that Italy was one of our enemies, extreme security measures were taken by the government, called for mainly by the fact that our region stood at the border with Italy. Not only were entire villages moved North, but 'suspects,' that is Italian sympathizers, were identified by the military police all over the Trentino. The less serious cases were confined to house arrest (*confinati*), the most serious were moved to concentration camps, such as Katzenau near Lienz or Mautern over Vienna, awaiting trial (*internati*). Within the larger frame of the European war, our internal conflict between the two languages, the German and the Italian-speaking Tyrol, became more complex than ever before.

§ § §

Gino's brother Tullio had first been given 'house arrest,' then submitted to a physical examination, drafted, and sent as a soldier to Lublin. He was betrayed by a local spy for his anti-Austrian activities, and sent to the camp of Katzenau. At least when Gino's turn came, Siora Maria was with him together with me.

§ § §

"Sior Gino is our savior," I often heard the women saying as they washed their linen at the public fountain in Tajo, "but if he doesn't pay attention he'll be caught in the web, whisked away, and we'll be left alone without much chance of survival."

The parish priest came to me personally to beg me to make Gino listen to the voice of common sense. Was this 'love for Italy' or for humanity at large worth the price he risked paying? The village needed him and loved him and nobody among the villagers could stand anymore the sight of his walking the tight rope.

My beloved Gino, mainly because of his nature, but also because of his knowledge of the world and of human psychology, his natural linguistic abilities and the authoritative position of his own family in the Valley, had become in recent months the key person in maintaining the precarious equilibrium of conflicting forces in our daily life.

In Tajo, a Military Command took care of the formation of the units to be sent to the front. From the onset of the war, Tajo enjoyed, as Gino put it, the privilege of serving as gate to the slaughterhouse. In the middle of the Church Square a big Altar had been erected where Mass was celebrated several times a day and the departing soldiers blessed and given the last rites reserved for the dying.

The soldiers accompanied the rite with songs in different languages, to each unit its own song. Their baritone voices vibrated through the stifling summer air filled with the love of their homeland, a last nostalgic call to their wives and children, mostly with such an intense desire for life that villagers, encouraged by Gino, gathered around them. We prayed for those soldiers who happened to be sent to our village from the unknown countries where our dear ones were sent to die. And while we prayed for them we seemed to forget how we hated them for *they* were the cause of the death of our village.

§ § §

On August 17, 1915, as Gino sat, "*Corriere della Sera*" in hand, among a group of soldiers, trying to answer their questions, two policemen approached him and declared him under arrest. They held the "Corriere della Sera" as evidence of the 'crime' for which he was to be deprived of his freedom.

On August 18, a national Austrian holiday, the anniversary of the inauguration of Franz Joseph, Siora Maria's personal maid Rosa reached me at home with a one line note: "Please come to see me. Enter with Rosa quietly from the farmers' courtyard." I found Gino sitting in his living room with Siora Maria near him. He had been informed that he should prepare to leave immediately for an unknown destination. He would be tried for crimes he had committed against his country.

Gino was his usual self-controlled, smiling self. Holding my hand in his, he assured me that the crimes of which they were accusing him, as far as he knew, were non-existent. They held against him, for instance, Siora Maria's prank on the Austrian police years earlier on the occasion of the Crown Prince's visit to the village. At the time, Gino was living as an American citizen in Cincinnati.

On August 19, Rosa brought me another brief message: "My departure for Lienz has been delayed by two days. Intervention through Mamma by friends in Vienna…."

We spent most of the two days sitting side by side on the sofa in the living room. I held Gino's hands in mine. His hands were cold and sweaty. He coughed and had difficulty breathing. Towards evening of the second day, close to the moment of his departure, Siora Maria called me into her bedroom. I was stunned by her appearance: a pale face without make-up, cut through by deep wrinkles, a red rose in her dyed hair, she wore the mask of pain. She could hardly speak. All I could make out from her rambling was that she was afraid of a recurrence of tuberculosis.

Gino discovered us embraced in tears. He smiled:

"I leave in your hands," he said to his mother, "my most precious treasure. Promise me you'll take care of her for the love of me." She promised and he embraced her. As he held me in his arms he whispered in my ear: "Never doubt for a moment that I'll be back. Nobody can stop us from building the happiest of all families...."

I believed deep in my heart every word he said. We separated without tears. I had shed all of my tears during the night before his departure, standing helpless with Speranza and Emma near the crib of Damiano's baby. He was eight months old, a lively creature who had enlightened our lonely black evenings as we huddled together, locked in the kitchen for fear of the soldiers. An epidemic of typhoid fever was taking its toll among us civilians, after having decimated the soldiers around us. Sick soldiers were taken to hospitals. We were left to die at home without any assistance. Damiano's baby died at dawn in Speranza's arms.

§ § §

Gino had warned me that for a while at least it would be hard for him to communicate with anyone. He would, however, write to me as soon as he could. Siora Maria and I kept in close contact. We took comfort in each other, two unfortunate women sharing the same miserable fate, the loss of the human being we most loved.

She was the first to get news a few weeks after his departure for "Lienz." He was interned in the camp of Katzenau among the swamps of the Danube, close to Lienz, she discovered through the grapevine of her connections in Vienna. He lived in a wooden hut, with a plank for a bed and a bowl of soup per day. He needed blankets and bread. The Austrians were starving. Could she provide a mattress, a blanket and some bread?

A month or so later Siora Maria discovered from the same source that the Danube had flooded the camp. Gino had survived for three nights and three days without food standing on the plank he used as a bed. Could she provide food and medicine...? He had a bad cough and temperature.

Sometime after that he was transferred to a Camp at Mautern near Vienna. Siora Maria had sent a mattress, a couple of blankets and some food to Katzenau. She was trying to discover whether he had received them in Mautern. No news directly from Gino. We lived off the bits and pieces we could pick up here and there from relatives of other prisoners. The two of us — Siora Maria and myself — took great comfort in being together, talking about him and praying for him, kneeling on a bench in the deserted little church of Santa Maria.

§ § §

One gray morning cousin Beppi, Mare's nephew, sent a note to me in school. Cousin Beppi was one of the most active persons in our community. As the station-master of Tajo, he lived with his wife and twelve children in a sprawling new one floor house at the newly built streetcar station. From there he took notice of every civilian entering or exiting his domain. On that gray fall morning he had rushed one of his twelve children to my classroom with a note bearing the news I had dreaded all along.

That very morning Siora Maria's daughters had arrived by streetcar from Trento and rushed to the mansion. Shortly after, the two ladies showed up again at the station with their mother and a couple of suitcases, in time to board the next streetcar back to Trento. The two sisters hardly greeted him. Siora Maria looked like a frightened bird, a little black hat over her uncombed black hair.

The news, under normal circumstances, would have stunned me. That very morning cousin Beppi's detailed note, which he had dictated to one of his young daughters in a rambling style, while busy managing signals, klaxons, or fixing rails, was for me a call to reality.

The paper on which the note was written in the best handwriting of one of my best students (who was, besides being my second cousin, also my godchild), bore all over it the stains of the kitchen whence it came. As I opened the envelope, from the oily paper the special smell of a household rose, a household teeming with exuberant children who screamed and laughed and cried hanging onto the long skirt of their plump, matron-like mother. I would have recognized that scent at a distance because I had known it all through my life, like Mare's voice and her own strong unique smell. The smell of food and dirty children that the page exuded was *home* for me. The kitchen of the *stazioneri* had retained, in spite of all misfortunes brought by the war, the liveliness that my own kitchen had lost, the life that mainly children can give, children who cry and laugh and play and scream and want attention. Children who want to be loved. I loved that kitchen as I loved my village.

§ § §

I knew that Siora Maria and Gino loved my village, but they didn't belong to it as I did. Body and soul. They had travelled and known the world. I hadn't. The village was my *only* home. Siora Maria could escape to Trento. I had no escape. I was now happy to share the fate of my village.

While I opened, read and then folded Beppi's note and placed it in my pocket, the little girl who had written it and brought it to me, who was named Gina for the sake of Gino, kept her black, intense, almond-shaped eyes fixed on me. She slightly rocked her slim frame back and forth, waving behind her a thick black braid that reached down to her hips.

"Thank your father for the information," I told Gina with a smile. "We all know that Siora Maria could no longer stand the harshness of our life in Tajo. But *we* can stand it by sticking together, right?"

"No!" the little girl rebuked me with firmness. "We *cannot stand it* anymore. Aunt Orsola told me we cannot, we should not stand it, and she is always right." Thus I discovered that Mare was again on the warpath.

§ § §

As war was fought in the trenches a few miles away from us, hundreds and hundreds of soldiers were billeted on the villagers. Every house was filled to capacity. In our own house the Command had requisitioned the whole whip workshop and the hayloft for soldiers, two out of our four rooms for officers — that is all of the house except the kitchen, the *stua* and a room on the second floor adjacent to the hayloft. Soldiers slept on straw laid on the workbenches or on hay. A given group of soldiers stayed with us for two, three, ten, or even fifteen days before being sent to the front.

The soldiers owned the village, that is everything on which they could lay their hands, they ate the fruit and vegetables of the orchard, and purely out of spite filled the fruit orchard in front of the house with their excrement, although they could have used the latrine built for their use. They kept to themselves and spent much time painting their horses the color of the earth. That, I remember, was their main occupation.

Most of those soldiers understood neither Italian nor German, least of all our dialect. Every new group spoke a different language. I had counted six or seven languages — with the help of Gino when he was still with us. Through the variety of their languages I marveled at the composition of our Empire. Each group stood by itself. All soldiers resented the war. Most, for some reason, hated the Italians.

Gino's presence among us had somewhat helped me to stand the sudden invasion of our lives, accept the soldiers as human beings, share their misery as we shared the same destiny. We were all victims of war. Far from their homes they were made to fight and die for no understandable reason, crushed by forces beyond them. Without Gino, I suddenly felt insulted by their very presence not to say by their behavior. Everything about them was an offense to my dignity. I knew I was wrong and, to the best of my ability, I tried to keep myself from hating them. Most of the time, however, my instinctive reeling from their overbearing attitude towards us was stronger than my reason. I knew also that most of the villagers resented them because they were so different from us. They killed the very soul of our village with their lack of respect for our own way of living. And I was now more than ever before an intimate part of my village.

Every night before falling asleep I turned with all my love to Gino and to God for help and guidance. But Gino was far away, breathing the air of a world unknown to me. Every day without news he moved a little farther away than the day before, not from me, but from the world I lived in. With time, I learned to believe in Gino's existence, like in God's, by faith.

At home, we lived locked in the *stua* or in the kitchen. At night I locked myself with Felice and Speranza in the room near the hayloft, lulled to sleep by the snoring of the soldiers. The smell of excrement raising from the fruit orchard was unbearable day and night, a constant reminder of the loss of our human dignity. Some groups of soldiers were more offensive than others. Neither God nor Gino helped me to stand all soldiers always with the same degree of patience. Neither God nor Gino helped me to bear the invasion of our home by the Serbs from Bosnia and Herzegovina.

One night, Speranza and I, locked in our little room upstairs near the hayloft, were busy trying to restrain four year-old Felice, who was from infancy as stubborn as a mule, from going downstairs. The two of us had spent a good part of the day in a far-away field digging out of the dry earth a few meager turnips, the only food for our daily family dinner. Hungry and exhausted, we had finally fallen asleep, when the cows with their mooing in the stable under our room signaled danger.

Soon after, we heard the Serbs knocking with the butts of their guns at the door of the *stua* near the kitchen where Mare slept with Emma and Silvio. We heard Silvio insulting them from behind the door. We knew, Speranza and I, that we should at all cost stop Silvio, whom we had managed to miraculously bring back home, from getting into a fight with the Serbs and thus coming to the attention of the police. Mare had little influence on Silvio. Emma even less.

With Speranza's help I stepped over the window sill, jumped into the hayloft, walked carefully between the bodies of the snoring Serbs, reached the kitchen, established communication with Silvio through a hole in the wall between kitchen and *stua*, convinced him to quiet down, waited in the kitchen until the first beam of light, and then stepping cautiously in between the bodies of the snoring Serbs who were blocking the door of the *stua*, headed straight to the Police Officer Goio.

Goio patiently heard my story. Then he gave me a long explanatory lecture on the nature of our guests. These were not common Austrian soldiers. They were exceptions. Didn't I notice that they were not asked to attend mass? That they prayed on their own, each on a small rug, those who had one, and sat usually cross-legged, smoking long pipes? Didn't I observe that they were more irascible than the other soldiers? Even he, the great Goio, felt uneasy in their company. What was wrong with them is that they were Muslims, not bad per se but certainly different from us....

I listened patiently.

"Muslims or not," I interjected with the authority of my position of teacher in the 'people's schools' of the Empire, "they are now Austrian soldiers, and nothing excuses their behavior. They have 'transgressed' those very rules the Army had established for them."

As I spoke out, however, I felt uneasy because Silvio was probably the only young man allowed to stay home in the whole village. And Goio was aware of it.

"I understand your point, Mr. Goio, and leave it up to you...." I concluded in a conciliatory tone. He courteously accompanied me to the door. Next morning Bosnia and Herzegovina were transferred from our home to the ground floor of townhall, placed under the very eyes of Mr Goio! On another occasion, I did not even have to appeal to Goio. I pushed the 'transgressor' out of my window. He fell with a thump to the ground below, broke his ankle and never reported me to the authorities. Gino would have been proud of me.

§ § §

As I lived drowned in a sea of soldiers in my village, I often remembered the days Gino and I had spent in Bolzano trying to save Damiano. The memory of Gino's elegant acrobatics with the military and the police juxtaposed to the image of a Damiano, clumsy in a new uniform too tight for his huge body, led me to an awareness of the awkward imbalance between us and the soldiers. I was free to act as I wanted, hurt but free, whereas the soldiers were nailed down to their fate. I often saw in my nightmares that monstrous train disappearing in a cloud of black smoke and Damiano's big hand waving. I woke up startled, feeling deep down in my soul a surge of empathy for all soldiers, helpless victims of a fate we all shared.

§ § §

An Austrian major had been staying forever and ever in our 'room in between.' He was a very sad looking middle-aged man who spoke perfect German in a low tone and avoided all company. He lived as if nobody existed around him. Every single night, without exception, he got himself drunk with bottles of Italian grappa he had brought back from the trenches.

At that time, I was sleeping in the *stua* with Mare and Silvio who claimed he had to 'protect' me as the young woman in the family. The truth was that it always fell upon me to protect him. He was an impulsive stubborn young man who often risked our lives together with his own.

One night we were awakened by the usual noise, the butt of a gun on the door of the *stua*. Our Major, in a state of total drunkenness exacted that the door be opened. Before Mare and I could stop him, Silvio was up, ready to challenge whoever was on the other side of the door. He knew it was the Major. What an incongruous situation! Silvio, a simple soldier on a precarious leave from the front, was challenging an Austrian officer, a war hero, a chest full of medals…. Mare and I tried in vain to bring Silvio to his senses.

From the *stua,* Silvio was cursing the Major in a mixture of *noneso* and German, the Major answering from the other side of the door in eloquent, passionate German. Finally, the Major lost his patience, pulled out his revolver, and warned us he was ready to shoot through the door. Silvio, totally out of control, laughed: "Try it!"

Mare, terrified, placed herself between Silvio and the door trying to shield her son from the bullet. In despair, I screamed for help. Our neighbor, the old Catina, heard me. She woke her own Major, the one billeted in her house, a quiet man who avoided alcohol as the cause of trouble. Catina's Major ran down, got hold of our

Major by the shoulders — as we could see through the keyhole — spoke to him gently and led him away.

The next day, Catina's Major caught me as I was heading for Goio to have our Major removed from our house. He begged me to forgive and forget. The war, he told me, was a terrible thing. It radically transformed a human being. It deprived him of all dignity. His poor comrade had been totally destroyed as a human being by his long stay in the trenches. Did I know what it meant to be suddenly ordered out of the protective shelter of the trenches, to be forced to run in the open under enemy fire into enemy lines? All of your friends die around you and you feel guilty, when the attack is over, to be one of the few who have survived. Seeing all of your friends die around you after you ordered them to get out of the trenches.... You, survivor by chance, are then declared a hero against your will. Your chest full of medals, you spend the night in nightmares, asking yourself silly questions to which there are no answers. There are no answers to the crimes committed in war.... Our Major was the survivor of horrible experiences. He lived in constant fear of being sent back to the trenches...

Catina's Major stopped and looked at me straight in the eyes: "Think," he said with tears in his eyes, "what your action implies...."

I was taken aback, stunned. Nobody, not even Gino, had ever brought to my eyes with such vividness the life of a soldier at the front. How could we live in the dark of what was happening a few miles away from us? I was embarrassed and ashamed. Gino's words in Sirmione echoed within my soul. I took the hand of Catina's Major into mine and swore to him I would never denounce his friend.

Next day our Major was sent to the front. He walked away from us, as he had come, in a trance. I was angry at whoever had denounced him and I cried for his departure as if he had been my own brother.

§ § §

As summer gave way to fall and fall to winter, we slowly learned how to live surrounded by soldiers. Soldiers swarming around us like flies. Soldiers filling every empty space. Soldiers unbreached in front of the kitchen windows emptying their bowels and laughing at us because we couldn't help looking at them. Soldiers smoking long cigars and throwing them at us in jest. Soldiers overflowing with lice. Soldiers so hungry they would eat the core of the cabbages we left in the field. (More than once I gave up my meager food so as not to be obsessed by their hungry look.) Soldiers trembling with fear. Soldiers cursing. Soldiers praying God to make them die before they were sent back to the trenches. Soldiers cursing God. Soldiers wanting to make love at all cost in order to forget, restrained by fear of punishment. Soldiers crying....

I often cried with them. And as I cried, I longed for my beloved Gino who had vanished into thin smoke. As month after month passed, the war became my own War because, in spite of my resistance, it was slowly dissolving the very texture of my own life. I then started to hate War blindly with an intensity that made me ill...

§ § §

I had the first premonition of my illness one day in Cles. I had walked to Cles from Tajo, almost a day's walk, to meet with the District Captain, one of Gino's old friends who had helped me with Silvio. Now I asked him to help me to contact Gino. Siora Maria had let me know that Gino had been placed in a hospital and was feeling better. I needed now to hear from him directly.

The Captain assured me he would get in contact with the officer in charge of both camps, Katzenau and Mautern, and communication with Gino would soon be re-established. When — he could not say —, but I shouldn't worry. Gino lived now on the shores of the blue Danube, a majestic river that ran through the middle of our beautiful Empire....

I knew he was trying to reassure me, but I was not in the mood to listen to his rhetoric on a beautiful river or on our Empire. I knew enough about our Empire from my soldiers at home.... All I wanted was Gino. Gino alive in my arms.

As I left the Captain's office, I felt weak and dizzy and asked myself where I was and for what reason I had come away from home. Where was home?

I regained my senses after I sat down for a while. It must be hunger, I thought. But I had nausea, a strong urge to vomit. Feeling too weak to walk back to Tajo, I hitchhiked on a military car. It was the first time in my life that I rode a car. Sick as I was, I enjoyed the ride.

I hardly made it to the big bed in the *stua*, called Emma, and she ran to me. "What happened to you, my sweet child?" she cried. She undressed me and tucked me into Mare's big bed. Soldiers were clamoring in the distance. Emma's gentle face was the last thing I saw before I entered darkness. Oh, how I loved Emma!

I think it was late fall or the beginning of winter when I fell ill. When I awakened, the birds were singing some place in the distance — or was I dreaming about them? Near a spring covered with soft moss violets bent their thin stems longing to touch the water. I was very thirsty. Emma was still holding my hand. Oh, how I loved Emma!

§ § §

Mare and Comare — I was told when I came to myself — given the gravity of my illness, had decided to report it to the Military Command. They begged to have me seen by a military doctor. I was immediately diagnosed with the worst case they had seen so far of typhoid fever, of which there was an epidemic among the soldiers. When I unexpectedly seemed to have conquered the typhus, my condition worsened because of a severe outflow of bile. More than once I was given up for lost and administered the last rites. During the period of three months I was most of the time unconscious.

As a special concession, the Command gave back to the family the use of one of our rooms, the 'room in between,' which was equipped for the occasion with a bed and the minimum of furniture to take care of a patient. A military doctor saw me whenever possible. The house was overflowing with soldiers. I was kept strictly separated from everybody. Emma and Speranza took turns caring for me. Mare said 'she didn't give a damn about catching my illness' and she spent long hours near my bed. Always in silence.

This happened — Emma told me in a low voice — while "I was away." Mare, she sadly concluded, had aged so much. She lived in a world of her own. She hardly ate or slept. And she hardly ever talked.

§    §    §

The first object that hit my eyes when I awakened from my slumber was the elaborate chandelier over my head. Where was I? Certainly not home. For a while I fumbled in the void, ambling in and out of houses I had known. Suddenly that chandelier produced the images of Siora Erminia and Siora Clementina, and Mare with them…. Mare.

Mare in her prime, young and powerful, ready to once more take charge alone of a family of six. Mare this time sadly willing to see one of her girls, out of the village boundaries, off into the unknown. Mare, straight like an arrow, her blond curly hair gathered in a knot over her head, dressed in her Sunday black uniform of thick coarse wool.

Mare is silent while Siora Erminia speaks, and a light breeze moves the curtain on the window open over the fruit orchard. As Siora Erminia speaks, Emma's lips tremble because she is afraid to leave the village, whereas Maria defiantly takes stock of her potentials, like a lion ready to jump on the prey, an old rich husband. Damiano and Silvio fight in the kitchen….

Why Emma? I tremble with Emma. Why should Emma leave us? I kneel among the cabbages in the orchard near the *pont*, and try hard to understand what Siora Erminia whispers to Mare, but I cannot make out the words. The church bells ring….

Sweet Emma lingers in my fantasy, young and beautiful with her decayed olive-skinned beauty, when suddenly Gino breaks the fog, strikes like lightning and I scream with pain. Emma leans over me. "Wake up!" she whispers. I open my eyes and notice the white streaks in her hair, the wrinkles in her face.

"Did Gino write? Are there some letters?" I utter my question with fatigue.

"There has been virtually no mail these past months. The war has been hard on us in many ways... I cannot tell you how hard... Whatever mail we got is in Mare's hands...."

I know Emma knows and doesn't want to tell me.

I fight hard to hold on with both hands to the brim of the pit, but I have to let go and I fall down deeper and deeper without touching ground. I can hardly breathe.

§ § §

Somebody holds my hand in hers. I know from the ruggedness of the skin it is Mare's hands. I open my eyes. My eyes meet Mare's and I know. There are no letters from Gino.

I feel like vomiting. With one hand Mare holds a pail, with the other my forehead. A flow of warm green bile fills the bottom of the pail. I feel empty and relieved. Tears flow freely now from Mare's eyes through the deep furrows running through her cheeks, down over my hand. I hear from the hayloft the harsh voices of the soldiers. They scream in a strange guttural language which is neither Italian nor German. I know I am alive. I try to lift my head from the cushions and faint.

§ § §

Emma and Speranza vie with each other in helping me to overcome my weakness. I lie for interminable hours on my bed looking at the clouds passing by. They are all hopelessly alike. Days go by, all alike, olive-stone grains in Mare's rosary.

Speranza makes me sip broth and milk. I ask her one day where and how she gets that broth and milk. Speranza laughs: "This is the best sign you are indeed coming back to us..." She kisses me sweetly as if I were her child, and sighs: "Finally."

I take her hands in mine and kiss them: "You are a Saint!" I whisper.

"Perhaps I am a Saint!" she echoes my words and in one breath she tells me how, almost by chance, one day early in March, while spring cleaning the *stua*, she discovered under Mare's mattress two bunches of letters, tied each not with a ribbon but with a coarse string. Out of curiosity, instinctively, she fumbled through the first bunch. They came from Katzenau and Mautern. With her heart throbbing at her throat she ran through the second bunch, of course without undoing the knot. They came from Mautern, Lublin and some other place she couldn't remember.

What are these letters doing here under Mare's mattress, Speranza asked herself. Probably Mare kept them if and when Beppina came back to us. But the day I had a relapse she heard from Mare at the dinner table: "I had to tell Beppina the *truth... There are no letters from Gino...."*

§   §   §

When the two precious bundles were brought to me and trembling, I opened with difficulty the first envelope, I discovered much to my dismay that I was too weak to read the letter I had waited for so much.

The letters were long and written in very small thin handwriting, the lines filling the page like ants in an ant-heap. The prisoner tried to fit in as much as possible onto one page. I had to stop after the first two paragraphs to regain strength. I asked Emma and Speranza to help me, but they had not read in years and could hardly read. They painfully went through a paragraph and then stopped like horses after a race, exhausted.

Besides, the reading had to be done at night, after Mare was asleep and only for a short time because electricity was cut off at 9:30 at the latest.

Every night, after the reading session, Speranza took back the precious bundles and kept them until the next evening under her own mattress in the room upstairs near the hayloft.

I was well aware I had to read those letters fast. The house was unsafe, overfilled with soldiers. The Italians had been defeated, they were fighting back. We were taking prisoners. Some Italian prisoners had even shown up in Tajo.

The greatest risk we were running was that Mare may look for those letters if new letters arrived. We carefully plotted to catch all new letters before they reached Mare. Speranza went to the post office early in the morning to catch a letter in time. At times she had to run back to the village from a field where she was working in order to do the job, but she was more than happy to deliver the precious document directly to me. She got to my bed breathless, with an angelic smile on her plain flat face. Still the problem of reading fast remained unsolved.

Finally, pressed by the urgency of the case, I gave in to a proposal by Speranza. We needed help in reading the backlog of correspondence. All three of us agreed that nobody in the village could be trusted to see those letters. But what about an Italian prisoner who, coming from far away, was totally in the dark about life in the village?

A young Italian prisoner from Modena with sparkling dark black eyes was chosen by Speranza for the purpose. He read aloud more letters to me in one hour than we had done in days. He read them in a low voice, in an effortless way. He could hardly hide his interest in some detail concerning strange places he had never heard of before and treatment of prisoners. At times, he stopped for a brief comment, but otherwise he was so discreet that when he got to a passage of an intimate nature, which was not very frequent, he stopped short and asked me to read it by myself later. Gino was aware that the letters were diligently censored by the military authorities. He therefore carefully censored his own letters before they fell under unknown, critical or at the least indifferent eyes.

When Speranza returned the stolen bundles to the place where she had found them — under Mare's mattress — I felt like myself again. To everybody's astonishment, I could take a few steps around the room, ate everything that was given to me, and slept all night long like an angel.

Mare was never aware we had discovered her secret. Speranza, Emma and I loved her so much we understood and accepted the reasons of her action. On one hand, she could not renounce for the sake of the family, not for herself, the benefits of my position in the village and the 700 yearly Kronen. On the other, although she dearly loved Gino, she thought he was too old and in feeble health to ensure the necessary support for my future family. She knew only too well by personal experience what supporting a family as a single parent entailed.

Finally she knew, not by experience but by ancestral wisdom, that in a village like ours, the boundaries between social classes were an accepted healthy measure to maintain our social equilibrium. Throughout the centuries, from Roman times on, — no matter who was their ultimate ruler, a German Emperor, the Archbishop of Brixen or more often the one of Trento, the Counts of Tyrol, Napoleon, or the Austrian Emperor — farmers had violently revolted at regular intervals against those social injustices that directly hurt them in making an honest living out of their fields. Their ultimate ruler was God and God's Son, Jesus Christ, who had died on the Cross precisely for them. They owed their ultimate loyalty mainly to God. Politics was a luxury for the Siori to enjoy.

Mare knew for instance —and was proud of it— that Maria Teresa in Vienna in 1774 had made public schools free and obligatory for everybody in the Empire. Farmers like her and her family were still enjoying the benefits of such a measure. Why should her children fight against Austria?

Mare was proud of being an honest farmer who had always owned her home. She enjoyed the respect of her peers in the village and of the Siori in their mansions. Had her daughter overcome that 'boundary,' Mare knew for sure she would have been exposed to unnecessary humiliations. She dearly loved Gino, his mother, his father, his aunts. But love did not play much of a role among harsh social considerations.

The war had given old Mare an opportunity to test Gino's motivations and mine to join our destinies after so many trials. She simply took advantage of that opportunity. That was the last great 'act' of her life before she entered the darkness she feared.

§ § §

I don't remember in detail the content of those letters. Gino, condemned to confinement and physical inertia, had not given up his instinctive curiosity. Since he could not touch upon any detail that concerned his trials and the consequent changes of residence, he limited his writing to what in his environment attracted his attention. Everything around him was of interest to him, his fellow prisoners, his guards, the history and the folklore around Katzenau, Mautern and Lublin, legends, children stories, the fauna and the flora, and mainly the mushrooms of the region, and of course the Danube, which he ironically called 'our Imperial River.' During the three and a half years of detention he wrote a little volume of local legends, a detailed description of local mushrooms, a Spanish grammar, and a comedy in Spanish.

For me those hundreds of letters had a value that went well beyond their content. They provided by their very existence the cement for my future life as Gino's companion. After having read them, I had no doubt whatsoever that Life belonged to the two of us *together*.

The underlying motif throughout all of those hundreds of pages was a secret anxiety that the writer tried hard to hide but couldn't. He had not received a single line from me. Why this silence? He openly expressed fear that something serious, beyond my control, might have happened to me. Yet, he had such blind faith in me and in my unconditional devotion to him that he never minimally doubted that if I existed somewhere in the world, I could, by sheer force of will, overcome all obstacles and join him, no matter where he was. And he let himself go to dreaming about our future life together, our children and their destiny, after the end of the war, in a world that, after the bloody inhuman experience with which the century opened, would have known a golden productive peace.

I also came into possession, much later, of some postcards Siora Maria was writing to her son. She wrote to him with infinite love and admiration for the way he had learned to survive his trials. But there was never a word about me.

I also found a picture-card of one of Gino's nieces, a daughter of his sister Clodia, which sadly confirmed to me what I knew well by 1917: Gino's family was still trying to detach him from me and

Siora Maria remained silent. In that picture card addressed by that niece to a certain Mrs. Baghetti Raisi, a co-prisoner of Gino's, the lady was encouraged to get closer to Gino. She was apparently a heroine of the Tridentine Resistance against the hated Austria. A much better candidate than me for marrying what Gino had become by now in the public eye, a hero of the Tridentine Resistance. The postcard, a photograph, reproduced a scene with which I was very familiar: Siora Maria and Gino walking arm in arm at "Fontanelle".

§ § §

In a document compiled by the District Captain of Cles, dated April 4, 1918, Gino's family was informed that their son was released from prison, and told how to get the appropriate permits to reach his home.

But Gino had been for the past months severely ill with Spanish influenza. People around him were dying by the hundreds. He wrote to me that he had to postpone his departure until he could stand on his feet. I felt sure he would make it. Nobody and nothing could stop us now from building together the family we had dreamt of for so long and with such intensity.

§ § §

During the year that followed my illness I slowly began to acquire a new awareness of life beyond the walls of my home, my village, my valley, and the century-long conflict between the two 'language groups,' Italian and German, in my own homeland. How it all happened I couldn't explain.

The evolution in my own personal view of life coincided with four years of a devastating war which slowly came to an end as if by exhaustion — with my own very experience of that war, as I lived it not at the front but in the "antechamber of the slaughterhouse, as Gino had defined Tajo in the summer of 1914.

During the interminably long time it took me to recover my strength — almost a whole year, that is up to the spring of 1918 — frustration and elation alternated, often leaving me in an anguishing state of mental and psychological confusion.

§ § §

When I reopened my eyes after months of darkness, I was as lost as a soul at its arrival at the deserted shores of the island of Purgatory. Life again, but at what price? The road ahead of me seemed anguishingly long and difficult. Gino's daily letters, which now Speranza delivered to me directly from the post office, behind Mare's back, were the indispensable ingredient of my will to live, of my fight for life. I don't know what would have happened to me had I not re-established contact with Gino.

§ § §

Why did Mare hide those letters in the first place? The question never surfaced within me when I could have rightly judged Mare's act as unjust, cruel and unnecessarily counterproductive.

I never judged Mare. Mare was for us women a natural phenomenon like the sun, beyond human judgment. It was not admiration we had for her. Her energy and strength were the source of our own strength. Silvio, the only male among us, so much younger than all of us, with his feet in our time and his head in the future, deeply loved Mare but resented her strength as an impediment to his own expansion in a world he always regarded as a challenge.

After my illness, I became aware of the difference in perception of life between Mare and myself. But I was not perturbed by that difference, because I had always accepted and respected Mare as she was. It was up to me to find my place near her.

There was, however, more to our relationship than an acceptance on my part of 'Mare's difference' from me. I never doubted then nor at any moment of my life that Mare and I, despite some radical differences between us, were indissolubly connected by the deep roots we shared. We both belonged to the same harsh dry earth that had kept alive generation after generation of our ancestors. I would always belong to Mare's world as long as I lived, no matter where and with whom I lived, as I belonged to my village.

Siora Erminia's and Siora Maria's equally deep attraction and love for both of us, Mare and me, implied an acceptance on their part that Mare and I belonged to the same world and yet were so different from each other. Two totally different flowers blooming from the same stem.

Gino went further than his aunt and his mother. He decided to tie his own destiny to ours, to allow two worlds to join forces.

§ § §

After my illness, at the very delicate moment when I had to face life as a "newborn," support for the continuation of my life came mainly from Gino. Gino at a distance, by force of his letters, became, during my convalescence, the role model of my life. And Gino brought with him a radically different world from the world of Mare; a world infinitely more complex which at first caused conflicts within me and at times anguishing perplexities. In the end, however, the two worlds came not only to a peaceful coexistence within me. In time, after Gino and I married and dedicated our lives to raising our children, and later when I was left alone to continue the work we had started together, it became evident that one world enriched the other.

While I slowly learned to stand for more than a few minutes without the friendly support of Speranza's arm, and then learned to walk, first around the room, then to the kitchen, finally down the *pont* on the road to Santa Maria, I instinctively acquired a new understanding of and an infinite admiration for Gino's efforts to regain his own strength again and again, illness after illness, under the restrictions his fate imposed on him — a fate to which, I could not help admitting, he personally contributed with his own actions — first alone on the other side of the Atlantic, then alone as a prisoner in a concentration camp. I read and reread his letters trying to detect hidden signs of weakness and bitterness, but there were none. I then felt puzzled, humiliated and at times guilty.

Why was I so much more 'lucky' than Gino? Was it because I didn't have the courage to live as he did, motivated by deep political convictions? Was it because all through my life I had stubbornly stuck to my family and to my village? In any case, since it was now to my family that I owed my life, I naively concluded that what Gino had missed all through his life was a family and the village to which the family belonged.

Near me throughout my illness, Emma, Speranza, and Mare had kept me alive by the sheer force of their love. Without their love I would have died. What did I do to deserve such a love? What was I doing now for them? I was asking for more. My first obligation was now towards my family.

As this thought flickered through my mind, I straightened myself out and forced myself to walk five, ten, twenty steps further on the path to Santa Maria. More than once I fell. When a friend lifted me from the ground I insisted on continuing to walk by myself. For a long time, I explained, I had been a weight on those who loved me. I had now resolved to quickly get back on my feet so that I could earn a salary.... Besides, nobody but me could help Silvio....

Silvio had been 'drafted' again while I lay unconscious on my back in 'the room in between' under the beautiful chandelier. He wasn't home when I opened my eyes to the world. What did Gino tell me up in Bozen when we tried to save Damiano? Dry your tears and help me to save him. War is like a fire... And now my thoughts wandered back to Gino....

That fire was still burning, today like yesterday. Franz Joseph, the Emperor Gino hated, had died, but his army was still now, in 1918, fighting the war of 1914. For us, his helpless subjects, nothing had changed. The war called for more and more men to the many fronts our new Emperor was forced to keep open.... Franz Joseph had died, but the war continued as before.... How could I help put an end to the war? Every citizen has the duty, Gino used to say.... Gino, Gino, Gino. Gino constantly calling me to order. I was terrified because I could not remember Gino's words any more.... I must at all cost make the effort to remember and act accordingly.

It was a sunny morning. I was most painfully striving to reach Santa Maria from my home, when I suddenly felt an urge within me to turn against the injustice of that war. I had heard what was happening in Russia, a revolt of the soldiers, of the workers, of the farmers... What could I do to help? I must force myself to think of life outside the walls of my home and my village. I must learn to think politically... Gino was in Lublin now, lost in the thick mist of the plains that lay North of our mountains. Unreachable. What could I do to help stop the nonsense of a war that kept us apart?

I was so weak I could hardly hold on to one thought before another thought overshadowed the first. What saved me from being submerged by an anguishing frustration as to what kind of political activity I could pursue was an ancestral instinct of survival, the instinct that had kept Mare alive and her own Mare before her and the Mare of her Mare. I was the offspring of a family that for centuries had survived by digging potatoes and turnips out of an ungrateful earth.

That ancestral instinct for survival warded off the urge to act out my frustration through some kind of political action and steered me towards the sunny shores of more earth-bound, simple decisions. Although I shared with Gino an inclination towards Italy, I was not ready to fight for it as Gino and many others did. I had to get well as fast as possible in order to pursue what was reasonable for me, what I could do best, what I had done so far all through my life: continue my teaching.

Perhaps one of the reasons Mare had hidden Gino's letters from me through the months of my illness was the fear that, misled by Gino's "*irredentismo*," I would, if I had recovered, follow him and end up like him in a concentration camp. She also feared that the Austrian police may unjustly suspect me of political activities simply because of my relationship to Gino.

While I was still too weak to leave the room, my colleague, maestro Gabrielli, came to visit me in order to warn me. Months ago, he had seen my name placed high on Goio's list of candidates for deportation, accused of close ties to a dangerous political prisoner. "Politics," Gabrielli overheard Goio saying with a sarcastic laughter "was a dangerous game for farmers like us. We should leave it to the Siori who could afford it!" My illness had saved me.

I was strongly aware of Goio's sarcastic remark when, later during my convalescence, setting gladly aside all possibility on my part of any political engagement, I embraced with a sense of relief the decision of doing what I could do. First, I had to get back to my school and teach. Didn't Sior Augusto declame in beautiful Italian, caressing his white beard with his long fingers: "We are proud to entrust to you the education of our citizens of tomorrow...?"

Then I had to help Silvio... Then, in time, the war would miraculously end, and Gino would be with me....

Deep in my thoughts, filled with a new faith in myself, I was painfully walking the road as usual to Santa Maria one morning when my skies turned blue, all worries gone, swept away by the wind of a new sudden vision. Gino was with me as he had always been. Now as always. But now in an episode so far back in time I had almost forgotten about it.

It was a beautiful summer day. A little farmer girl running away from an impertinent boy who was pursuing her climbed one of the linden trees like a monkey near the old church of Santa Maria.

The girl challenged the boy: "Catch me now if you can!"

The boy: "Why should I catch you now? I'll get you anyway some day when you don't expect it!"

The girl: "How will you do that? You are too fat to climb a tree!"

The boy: "Thin or fat, I'll get you some day as my wife in this old church!"

§ § §

The very day I returned to my classroom I planned my visit to Gino's friend up in Fondo who was in constant need of butter. He acted surprised by my sudden appearance. Yet, given my gaunt looks, he accepted my excuses for the long absence and welcomed the package I unobtrusively left on a chair in his office.

Silvio was immediately transferred from the front to the police headquarters in Cles where this time he served as special assistant to the head officer. Given Silvio's long and varied experience with the Army of our Empire, his alertness and his innate ability to search for food when everybody around him was starving, coupled with his firm will not to die young, he was made special banquets chef and trainer of new recruits.

§ § §

At home, apart from Silvio's departure, nothing had changed. I closed my eyes, surrounded by hundreds of hungry derelict soldiers. After my recovery almost a year later, I spent my long months of convalescence in the company of hundreds of soldiers who dragged their feet day after day through the halls of my home, scratched their heads to the point of bleeding in a vain attempt to win a battle against lice, dug into the earth of our orchard with their bayonets in a futile search for a turnip or a potato of which a starving, luckier comrade who preceded them had deprived them. The only difference between then and now was that the soldiers around me today were the ghosts of those of once. It was hard to imagine how any of these soldiers could gather enough strength to approach the door of the *stua* with bad intentions.

Much had happened on the Italian front while I was 'away.' The Austrian Army, I was told, had defeated the Italians and chased thousands of soldiers in total disarray down through the peninsula. I asked myself with what kind of soldiers Austria had managed to break through the enemy lines. Certainly not with those billeted in our homes in 1917!

The hardest fighting, I was told, had taken place around a town called Caporetto, east of us, among the mountains of Carso in Venezia Giulia, until then unknown to us. Then the Italians acquired a new general, a certain Cadorna, I was told, who taught them how to fight. One unlucky day for the Austrians the Italians crossed a river called Piave, until then unknown to us, and marched victoriously north towards us.

And one night around midnight, the church bells rang furiously, echoed by the trumpets of the sentinels at townhall. We were ordered to quickly pack a few essentials for a long voyage north. We gathered, each with a small bundle, in Church and waited and waited. We first prayed then slept. I was still weak and fell asleep leaning against Speranza's wide soft shoulders. Lucifer was shining bright in the sky, when they told us to go back home....

Shortly after that night, something extraordinary happened. One morning at dawn our ghost-soldiers got up from the hay and started to move, with the bit of strength they still had, out of the village. Many of them leaving their arms behind in our homes, they headed out in long columns, as fast as they could, down the valley of the Noce, up the valley of the Adige, north through the Brenner Pass.

§ § §

When a young Italian officer, short, slim and lively, entered the village and told us we had been *liberated*, we welcomed him with open arms. We could not believe that after so many years those forlorn soldiers were gone forever and we could reacquire our homes for ourselves.

Yet it was so. The war had ended, the lieutenant said, and we could finally proudly call ourselves "Italians." Not all of us felt proud, but we were all happy. He had spoken eloquently, with tears in his eyes. I joined other young women to lead that young emotional Italian for a tour of the village. I knew that Gino would follow shortly after him, and I could hardly restrain my joy.

Shortly after the appearance of the Italian officer in the village, a haggard man slowly walked the short road that leads from Santa Maria to our home. He was leaning on a stick and looked too weak to make it to our *pont*. He stopped frequently, breathing heavily.

Emma was the first to recognize him. She ran to him, an old woman running like a young girl, held him tight in her arms and cried so loud we all moved out on the *pont*. Speranza was next over him and finally Mare led to him, kissed him on the forehead.

I was the last one to reach him. I still walked slowly and was easily out of breath. Gino held me in his arms for a long time without saying a word. There was nothing to say.

Our marriage took place shortly after the armistice, on November 25, 1918, in the little church of Santa Maria. In the presence of my family and Siora Maria, it sanctioned a union that had slowly materialized through our lives, cemented by the common experience of a war we had survived in unison from two different fronts.

# Epilogue

Maria, Giovanni, and Rina, with us in Tajo for the marriage, brought Gino and me down South which we once called "beyond the border," to Italy. As Italians, we had obtained a special passport that allowed us to move around the area that had been recently 'liberated.' While Gino and I spent our honeymoon in Sirmione, I often asked myself what it meant to be 'liberated,' a frequently used word in those days, to be an "Italian."

In Sirmione, I felt as if, by becoming "Italians," we had changed house and moved into a most spacious abode, with much more freedom of movement. I realized that the old 'border' had cut off my village from what was geographically its natural direction for expansion. That border had made it difficult for us to communicate with the South, with an Italy whose language was the root of the dialect we spoke. The high mountains behind us, while protecting us from the northern winds, signaled the geographical direction which would contribute best to our development. It took a war to make me and many others like me aware of this self-evident fact. By being allowed to communicate directly with the South, that is with Italy, my village stood a new chance of revival. It was a relief for Gino and for me to think that the spell was finally broken. We would not lose sight of a new Tajo, while the time had come to build a life together under new skies. Our marriage was greeted in the Valle di Non and in Trento as a signal of a new freedom from social conventions. A young Italy had succeeded an old Austria. We were admired and envied. We longed, however, for something else: a new challenge in a new world.

In 1919, Gino had been offered the directorship of an Italian Bank in Bolzano, the capital city of the German speaking former Austrian Südtirol. By inheriting the Südtirol with its German and Italian speaking population, Italy faced the nagging problem that Austria had faced until now: how to do justice to each of the two communities. For Gino, this was a most delicate but also very challenging problem that the Italians should tackle with an understanding of the basic needs of the group now risking to be sacrificed: the German speaking Tirol. The German language and culture of the old Tirol should be preserved as much as possible, while the land itself should rightly be an integral part of Italy, and its population Italian. Gino viewed himself as one of the persons best qualified to help the recently arrived Italians to carry out the task. Since it was out of the question for both of us, given our health, to cross the Ocean, Gino accepted the offer of the "Banca di Sconto." Bolzano would be our little America, a few steps away from my family, yet light miles away from the world we had overcome.

§   §   §

While we were enjoying life in Sirmione and preparing for the future, the Italian Comando nominated Gino *commissario* for Tajo and the adjacent area, a function he retained until March 1919. What would Sior Augusto have said if he had seen the son he had disinherited now invested by the Italian government with the highest official function in the area?

On the occasion, Gino spoke in front of Tajo's Town Hall where his father used to speak as a liberal, enlightened, pro-Italian member of the Vienna Parliament. Siora Maria and Gino's sisters and brothers, and their husbands, wives and children sat with me in the front row, a few steps from the stand erected for the occasion, among Italian *tricolori* and white and red flowers. The band played the Italian national anthem that most of us had never heard before.

I saved Gino's brief speech written in his beautiful handwriting, without a single correction. When he spoke I was overwhelmed by the joy of listening to his voice, rather than by the meaning of his words. It was a very emotional speech whose content does not make much sense out of the historical context in which it was delivered. In Tajo, in November 1918, the longing for Italy and the songs that went with it were as fresh and clean as a new-born baby. Old Austria was buried and a young Italy had replaced it.

Gino's speech stands out among his writings as the only expression of resentment for his own sufferings:

"Ladies and gentlemen, Mr. Mayor, Mr. Captain, Citizens!... While the Austrian guns roared at the front, on this side of the border the Austrian police... made an army of victims among us, the old and the young, men and women alike. By the thousands we were arrested, tried and condemned…Some of us condemned to death… I prefer not to remember. The wounds of the years spent in prison are still too recent for me to speak about…. Yet down there in the audience I see some of you acting as if the support of Austria were still behind them…. Shame on you. You belong to the past. Spies of Franz Joseph, I beg you to respect our sufferings of once and our joy of today…I beg you, leave us alone today…."

§ § §

In 1925, seven years after the end of the war, shortly before his untimely death, in a bleak moment of our lives, I asked Gino to read to me aloud that emotional speech. We had by then experienced together the fulfillment of our marriage: the happiness of bringing four children into the world, surrounded in Bolzano by love and by the full recognition of Gino's merits. We had also suffered together the bitterness of a recent severe political and business reversal.

Gino glanced silently at his writings. Then he laughed heartily as he used to in the old times: "Please spare me the effort of acting again like a hero. Once is more than enough!"

There was no bitterness in his voice and no regret. He had inherited from his mother the gift of a laughter that freed him from the world around him when it weighed too heavily on his shoulders. He could also laugh at himself when he ran the risk of being caught in the web of his own little world.

# About the Author

Born and educated in a classical school in the Alto Adige –Sudtirol between the two world wars, Maristella de Panizza Lorch earned a doctorate in classical philology in 1942 at the University of Rome with the Accademico d'Italia Professor Vincenzo Ussani, Sr.

After fifty years of teaching, she is Professor Emerita of Italian and Medieval and Renaissance Studies at Barnard and Columbia. Among her books: the critical edition of Lorenzo Valla's *De Voluptate* (1431-44), its English translation *On Pleasure*, the edition of Ziliolo Zilioli's *Michaelida* (1431), *A Defense of Life* (a study of Renaissance Epicureanism) and, with the philosopher Ernesto Grassi, *Folly and Insanity in Renaissance Literature*, an interpretation of humanistic literature and chivalric poetry. Albert Rabil's four volume collection of essays on Renaissance Humanism was dedicated to her in recognition of her promotion of Medieval and Renaissance Studies in America.

Maristella Lorch is known at Columbia for her courses on Dante, Petrarch, Renaissance Humanism, Renaissance Theatre, Machiavelli and Ariosto; in Europe, particularly Italy and France, as an active promoter of international exchanges. She founded and directed the Center for Medieval and Renaissance Studies, the Center for Italian Studies, the Center for International Scholarly Exchange, and the Italian Academy for Advanced Studies in America (1991). She founded La Scuola New York Guglielmo Marconi, was member of the Advisory Board of the Lycée Français de New York, Vice-President of EPIC (the fellowship of Emeriti Professors in Columbia), and a teaching faculty member in the M.A. in Liberal Arts Program at Columbia's Graduate School of Arts and Sciences.

Since 1996, as Founding Director Emerita of the Academy for Advanced Studies, she worked at the trilogy *Beyond Gibraltar*, a fictionalized memoir or *récit d'initiation*, based on her Euro-American identity, while at the same time offering courses for adults on Dante, Homer, Virgil, and Ovid. The first volume of that trilogy, *Mamma in her Village*, was first published by Ruder Finn Press, N.Y., in 2005 and republished by TBR Books in 2021. The second volume, *Beyond Gibraltar*, was first published in 2013 by Pegasus Press and republished by TBR Books in 2020. Finally, *The Other Shore* was originally published by TBR Books in 2019.

Maristella Lorch is the mother of three daughters and the widow of the mathematician Edgar Raymond Lorch. She divides her time between her homes in New York City and in Napanoch, N.Y.

# About TBR Books

*A Program of The Center for the Advancement of Languages, Education, and Communities (CALEC)*

TBR Books is a program of the Center for the Advancement of Languages, Education, and Communities. We publish researchers and practitioners who seek to engage diverse communities on topics related to education, languages, cultural history, and social initiatives. We translate our books in a variety of languages to further expand our impact. Become a member of TBR Books and receive complimentary access to all our books.

## Our Books in English

*Immigrant Dreams* by Barbara Goldowsky

*Rainbows, Masks, and Ice Cream* by Deana Sobel Lederman

*Can We Agree to Disagree?* by Agathe Laurent and Sabine Landolt

*Salsa Dancing in Gym Shoes: Developing Cultural Competence to Foster Latino Student Success* by Tammy Oberg de la Garza and Alyson Leah Lavigne

*Mamma in her Village* by Maristella de Panizza Lorch

*The Other Shore* by Maristella de Panizza Lorch

*The Clarks of Willsborough Point: A Journey through Childhood* by Darcey Hale

*Beyond Gibraltar* by Maristella de Panizza Lorch

*The Gift of Languages: Paradigm Shift in U.S. Foreign Language Education* by Fabrice Jaumont and Kathleen Stein-Smith

*Two Centuries of French Education in New York: The Role of Schools in Cultural Diplomacy* by Jane Flatau Ross

*The Clarks of Willsborough Point: The Long Trek North* by Darcey Hale

*The Bilingual Revolution: The Future of Education is in Two Languages* by Fabrice Jaumont

Our Books in Translation

*Rainbows, Masks, and Ice Cream* by Deana Sobel Lederman is available in 7 languages.

*Can We Agree to Disagree?* By Agathe Laurent and Sabine Landolt is available in 2 languages.

*The Bilingual Revolution* by Fabrice Jaumont is available in 11 languages.

*The Gift of Languages* by Fabrice Jaumont and Kathleen Stein-Smith is available in 3 languages.

Our books are available on our website and on all major online bookstores as paperback and e-book. Some of our books have been translated in Arabic, Chinese, English, French, German, Hebrew, Italian, Japanese, Polish, Russian, Spanish. For a listing of all books published by TBR Books, information on our series, or for our submission guidelines for authors, visit our website at

http://www.tbr-books.org

# About CALEC

The Center for the Advancement of Languages, Education, and Communities is a nonprofit organization with a focus on multilingualism, cross-cultural understanding, and the dissemination of ideas. Our mission is to transform lives by helping linguistic communities create innovative programs, and by supporting parents and educators through research, publications, mentoring, and connections.

We have served multiple communities through our flagship programs which include:

- TBR Books, our publishing arm; which publishes research, essays, and case studies with a focus on innovative ideas for education, languages, and cultural development;

- Our online platform provides information, coaching, support to multilingual families seeking to create dual-language programs in schools;

- NewYorkinFrench.net, an online platform which provides collaborative tools to support New York's Francophone community and the diversity of people who speak French.

We also support parents and educators interested in advancing languages, education, and communities. We participate in events and conferences that promote multilingualism and cultural development. We provide consulting for school leaders and educators who implement multilingual programs in their school. For more information and ways, you can support our mission, visit

http://www.calec.org

www.ingramcontent.com/pod-product-compliance
Lightning Source LLC
LaVergne TN
LVHW041253080426
835510LV00009B/714